TABLE OF CONTENTS

07 01

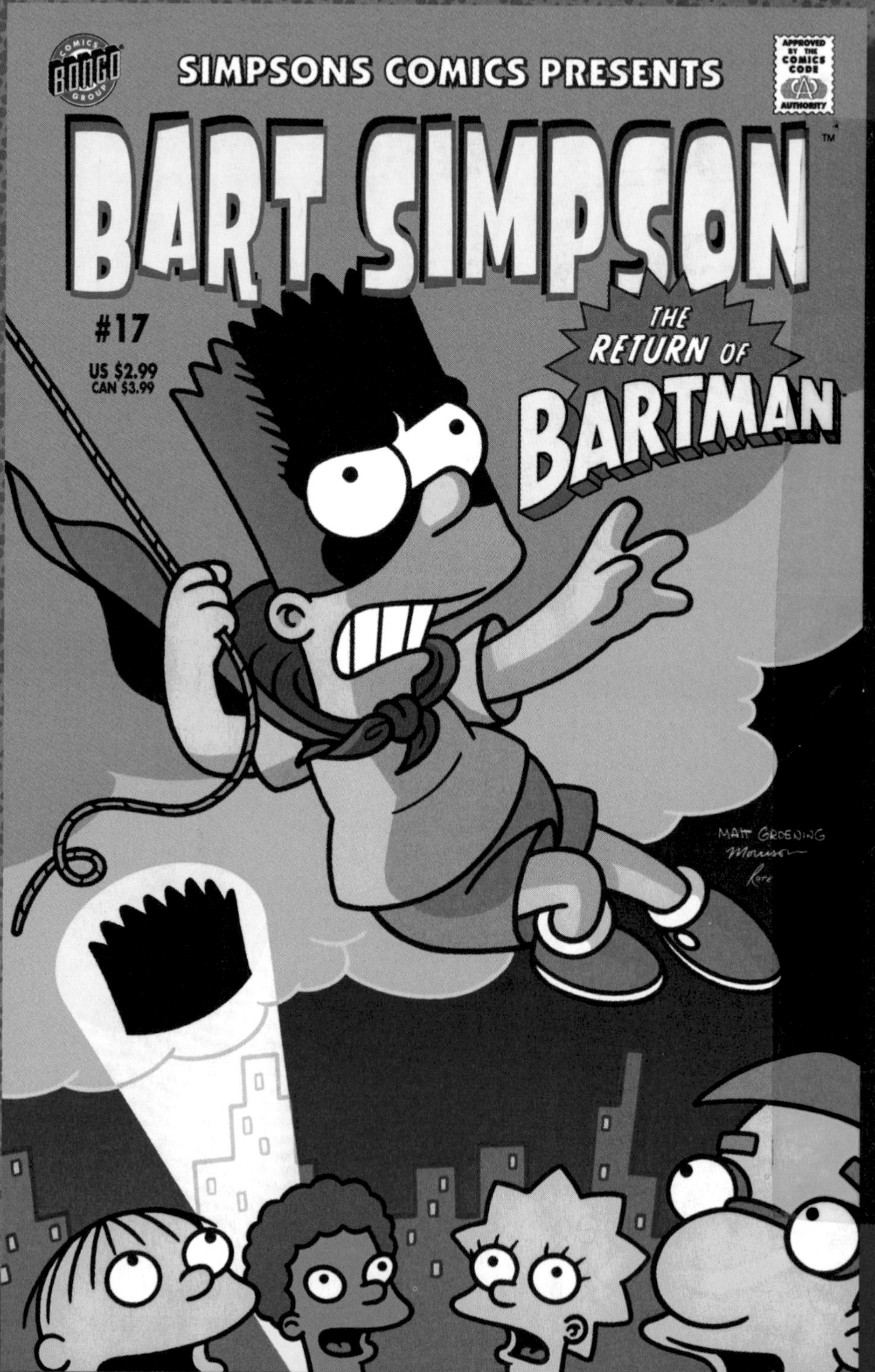

BONGO COMICS GROUP
SIMPSONS COMICS PRESENTS
APPROVED BY THE COMICS CODE AUTHORITY
BART SIMPSON™
#17
US $2.99
CAN $3.99
THE RETURN OF
BARTMAN
MATT GROENING

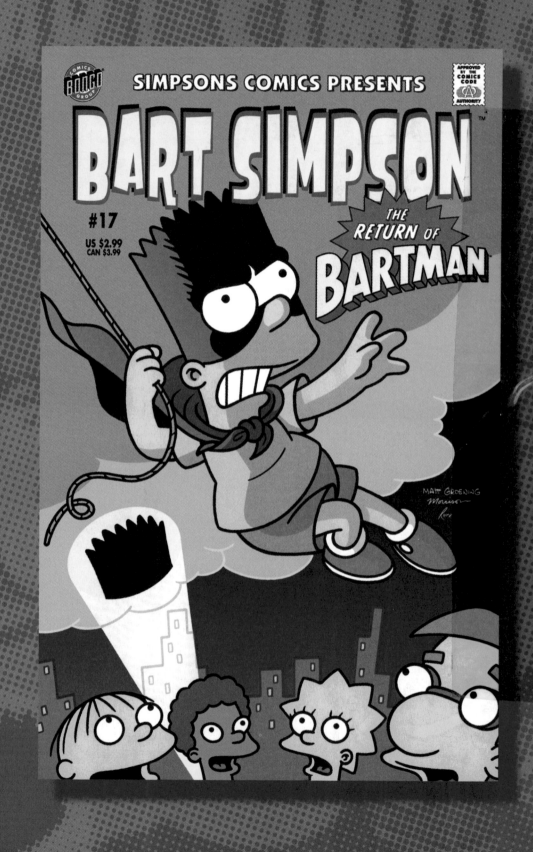

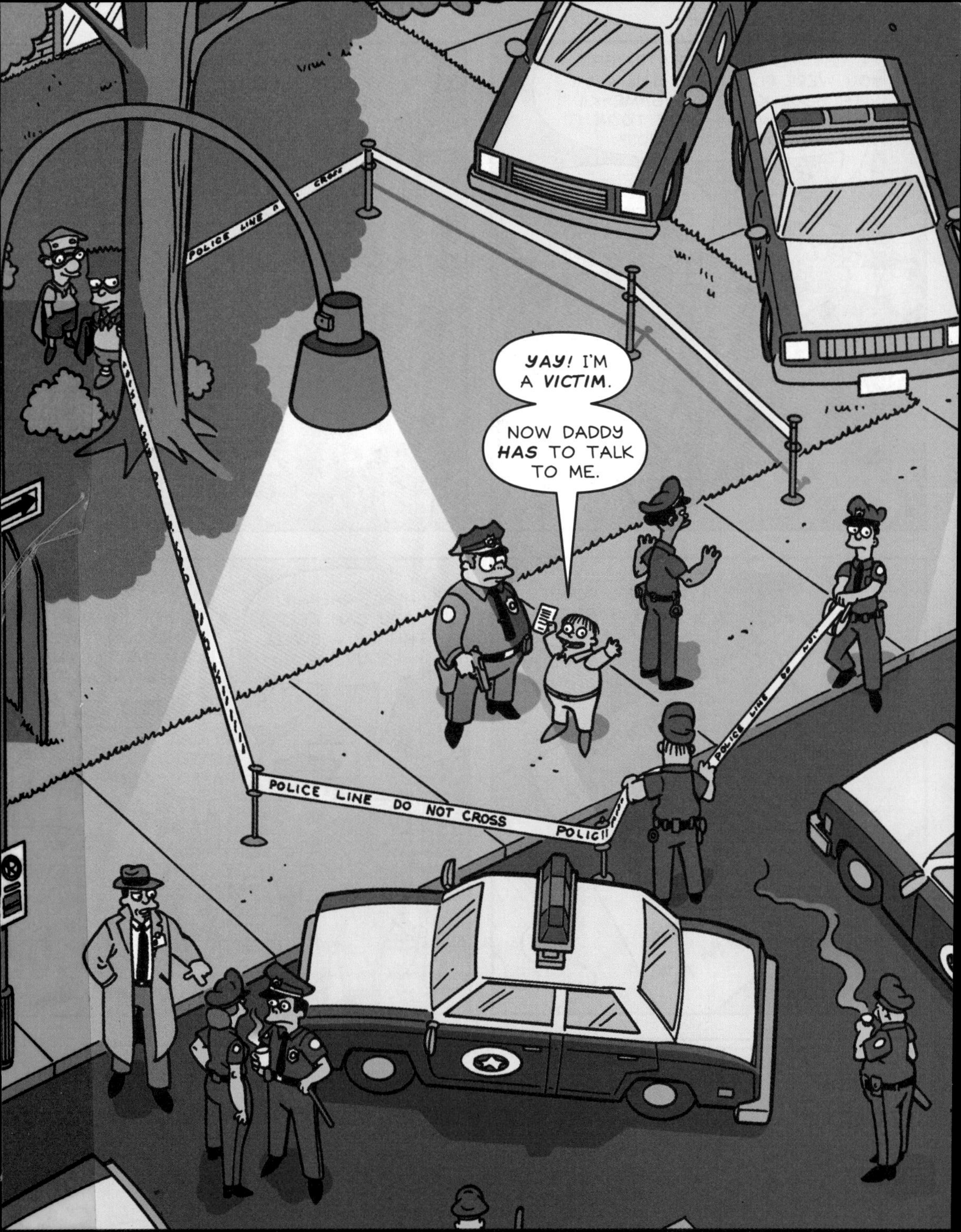
YAY! I'M A VICTIM.
NOW DADDY HAS TO TALK TO ME.
POLICE LINE DO NOT CROSS
POLICE

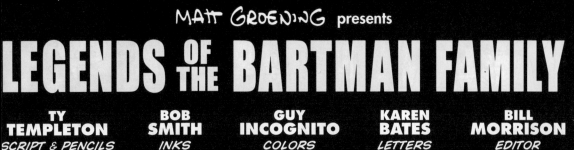

MATT GROENING presents

LEGENDS OF THE BARTMAN FAMILY

TY TEMPLETON
SCRIPT & PENCILS

BOB SMITH
INKS

GUY INCOGNITO
COLORS

KAREN BATES
LETTERS

BILL MORRISON
EDITOR

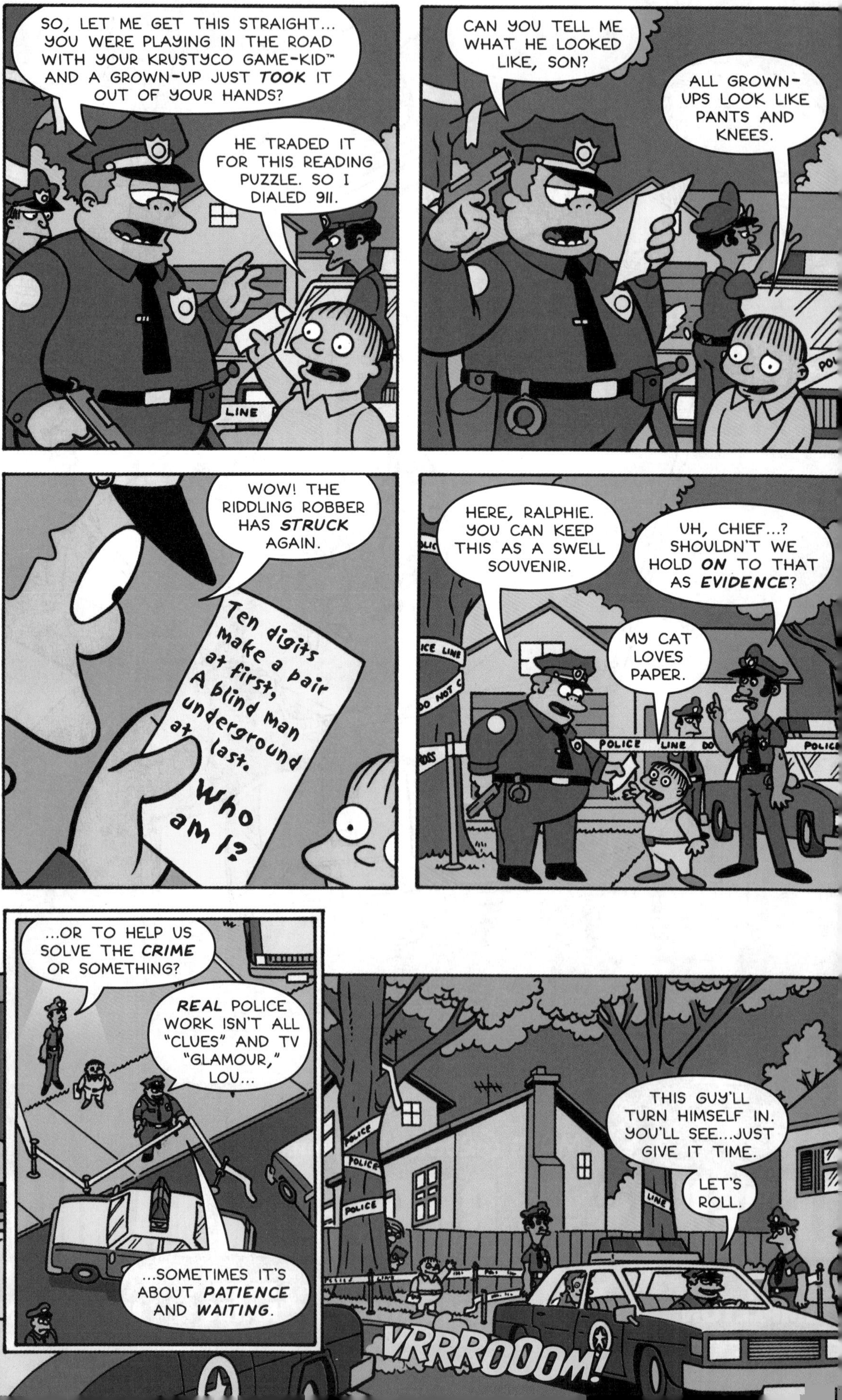
SO, LET ME GET THIS STRAIGHT... YOU WERE PLAYING IN THE ROAD WITH YOUR KRUSTYCO GAME-KID™ AND A GROWN-UP JUST *TOOK* IT OUT OF YOUR HANDS?
HE TRADED IT FOR THIS READING PUZZLE. SO I DIALED 911.
CAN YOU TELL ME WHAT HE LOOKED LIKE, SON?
ALL GROWN-UPS LOOK LIKE PANTS AND KNEES.
WOW! THE RIDDLING ROBBER HAS *STRUCK* AGAIN.
Ten digits make a pair at first, A blind man underground at last. Who am I?
HERE, RALPHIE. YOU CAN KEEP THIS AS A SWELL SOUVENIR.
UH, CHIEF...? SHOULDN'T WE HOLD *ON* TO THAT AS *EVIDENCE*?
MY CAT LOVES PAPER.
POLICE LINE DO
...OR TO HELP US SOLVE THE *CRIME* OR SOMETHING?
REAL POLICE WORK ISN'T ALL "CLUES" AND TV "GLAMOUR," LOU...
...SOMETIMES IT'S ABOUT *PATIENCE* AND *WAITING*.
THIS GUY'LL TURN HIMSELF IN. YOU'LL SEE...JUST GIVE IT TIME.
LET'S ROLL.
VRRROOOM!

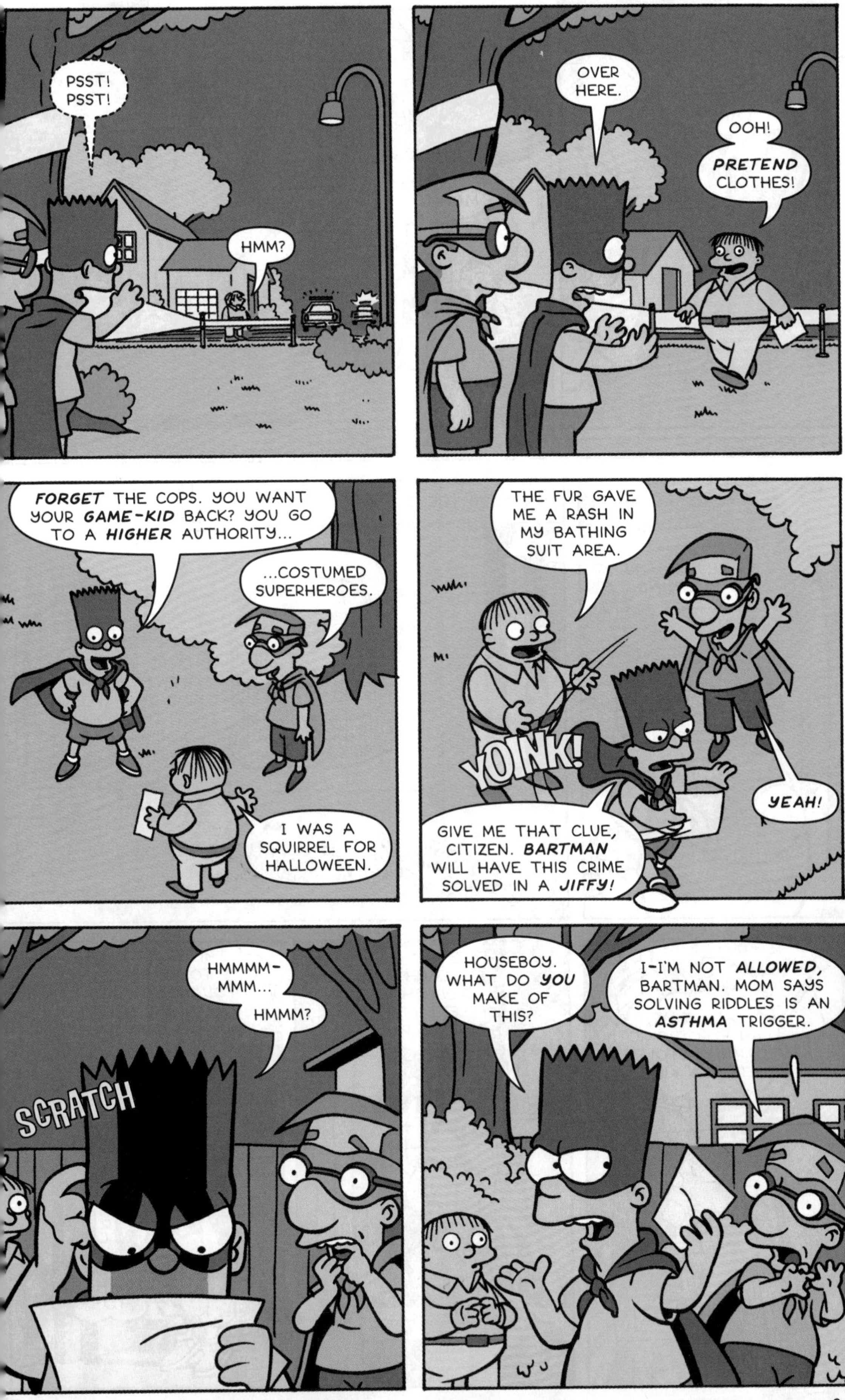
PSST! PSST!
HMM?
OVER HERE.
OOH! PRETEND CLOTHES!
FORGET THE COPS. YOU WANT YOUR GAME-KID BACK? YOU GO TO A HIGHER AUTHORITY...
...COSTUMED SUPERHEROES.
I WAS A SQUIRREL FOR HALLOWEEN.
THE FUR GAVE ME A RASH IN MY BATHING SUIT AREA.
YOINK!
GIVE ME THAT CLUE, CITIZEN. BARTMAN WILL HAVE THIS CRIME SOLVED IN A JIFFY!
YEAH!
SCRATCH
HMMMM-MMM... HMMM?
HOUSEBOY. WHAT DO YOU MAKE OF THIS?
I-I'M NOT ALLOWED, BARTMAN. MOM SAYS SOLVING RIDDLES IS AN ASTHMA TRIGGER.

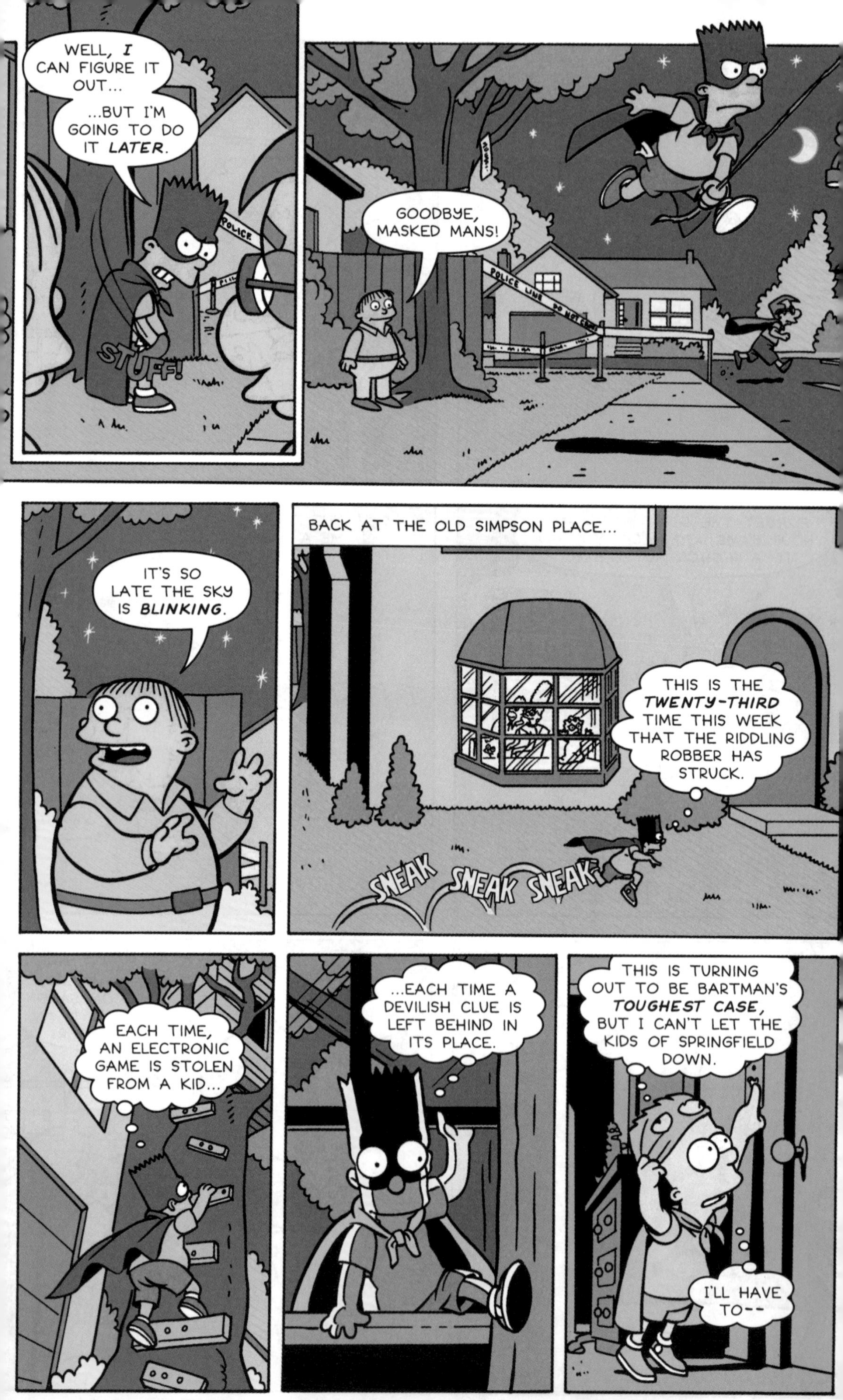
WELL, *I* CAN FIGURE IT OUT...
...BUT I'M GOING TO DO IT *LATER*.
POLICE
STUFF!
GOODBYE, MASKED MANS!
POLICE LINE DO NOT CROSS
IT'S SO LATE THE SKY IS *BLINKING*.
BACK AT THE OLD SIMPSON PLACE...
THIS IS THE *TWENTY-THIRD* TIME THIS WEEK THAT THE RIDDLING ROBBER HAS STRUCK.
SNEAK SNEAK SNEAK
EACH TIME, AN ELECTRONIC GAME IS STOLEN FROM A KID...
...EACH TIME A DEVILISH CLUE IS LEFT BEHIND IN ITS PLACE.
THIS IS TURNING OUT TO BE BARTMAN'S *TOUGHEST CASE*, BUT I CAN'T LET THE KIDS OF SPRINGFIELD DOWN.
I'LL HAVE TO--

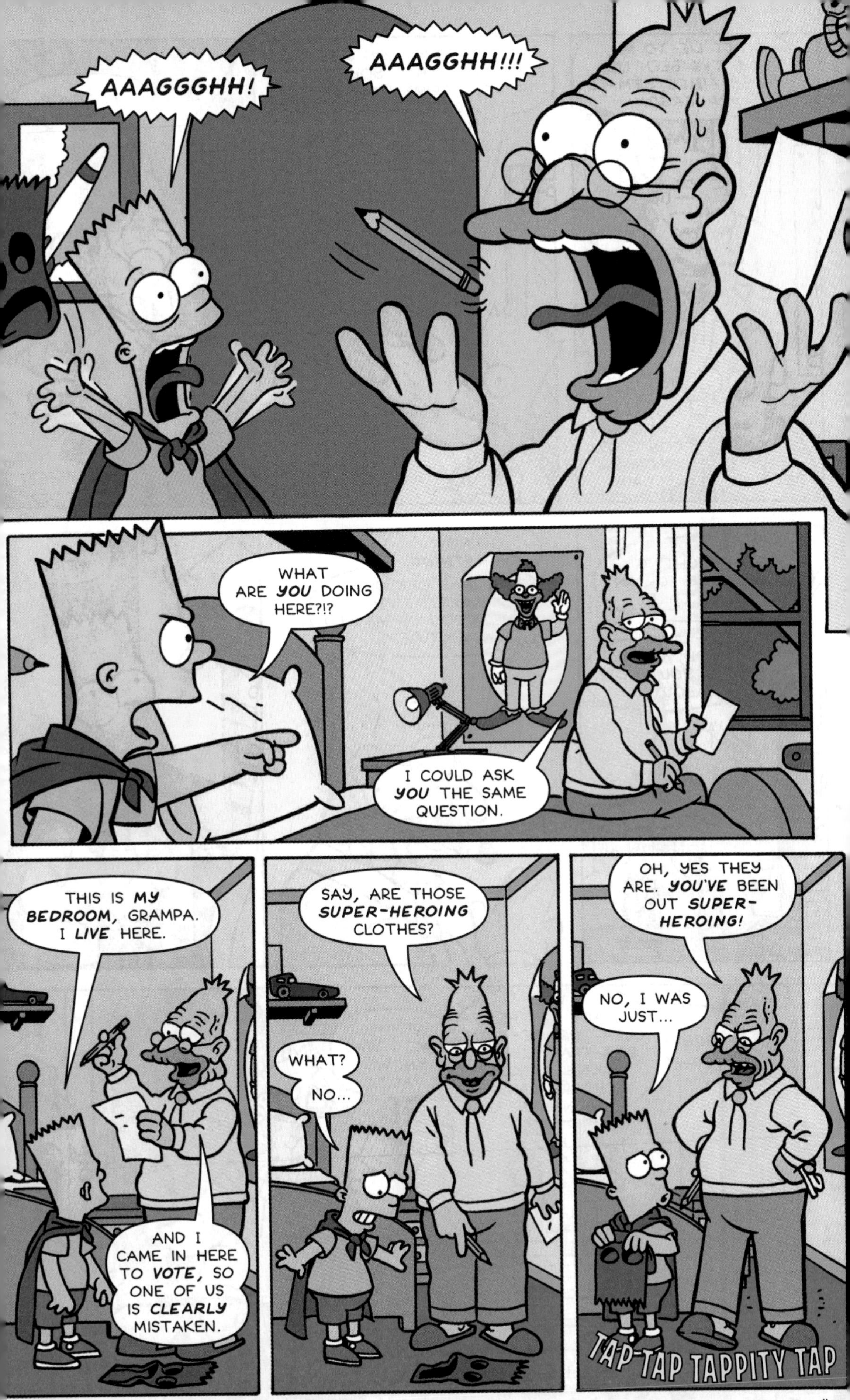
AAAGGGHH!
AAAGGHH!!!
WHAT ARE YOU DOING HERE?!?
I COULD ASK YOU THE SAME QUESTION.
THIS IS MY BEDROOM, GRAMPA. I LIVE HERE.
AND I CAME IN HERE TO VOTE, SO ONE OF US IS CLEARLY MISTAKEN.
SAY, ARE THOSE SUPER-HEROING CLOTHES?
WHAT?
NO...
OH, YES THEY ARE. YOU'VE BEEN OUT SUPER-HEROING!
NO, I WAS JUST...
TAP-TAP TAPPITY TAP

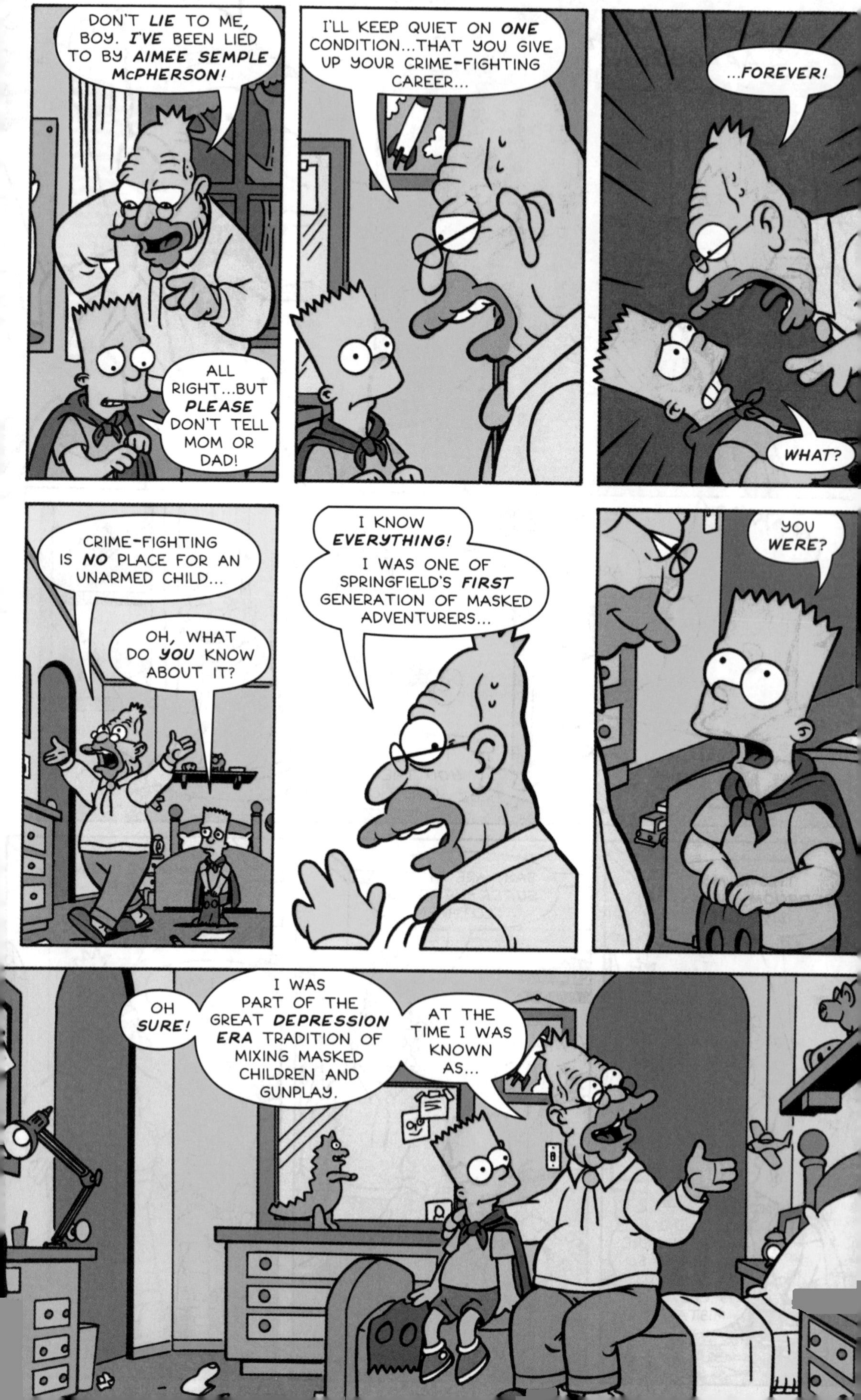
DON'T LIE TO ME, BOY. I'VE BEEN LIED TO BY AIMEE SEMPLE McPHERSON!
ALL RIGHT...BUT PLEASE DON'T TELL MOM OR DAD!
I'LL KEEP QUIET ON ONE CONDITION...THAT YOU GIVE UP YOUR CRIME-FIGHTING CAREER...
...FOREVER!
WHAT?
CRIME-FIGHTING IS NO PLACE FOR AN UNARMED CHILD...
OH, WHAT DO YOU KNOW ABOUT IT?
I KNOW EVERYTHING!
I WAS ONE OF SPRINGFIELD'S FIRST GENERATION OF MASKED ADVENTURERS...
YOU WERE?
OH SURE!
I WAS PART OF THE GREAT DEPRESSION ERA TRADITION OF MIXING MASKED CHILDREN AND GUNPLAY.
AT THE TIME I WAS KNOWN AS...

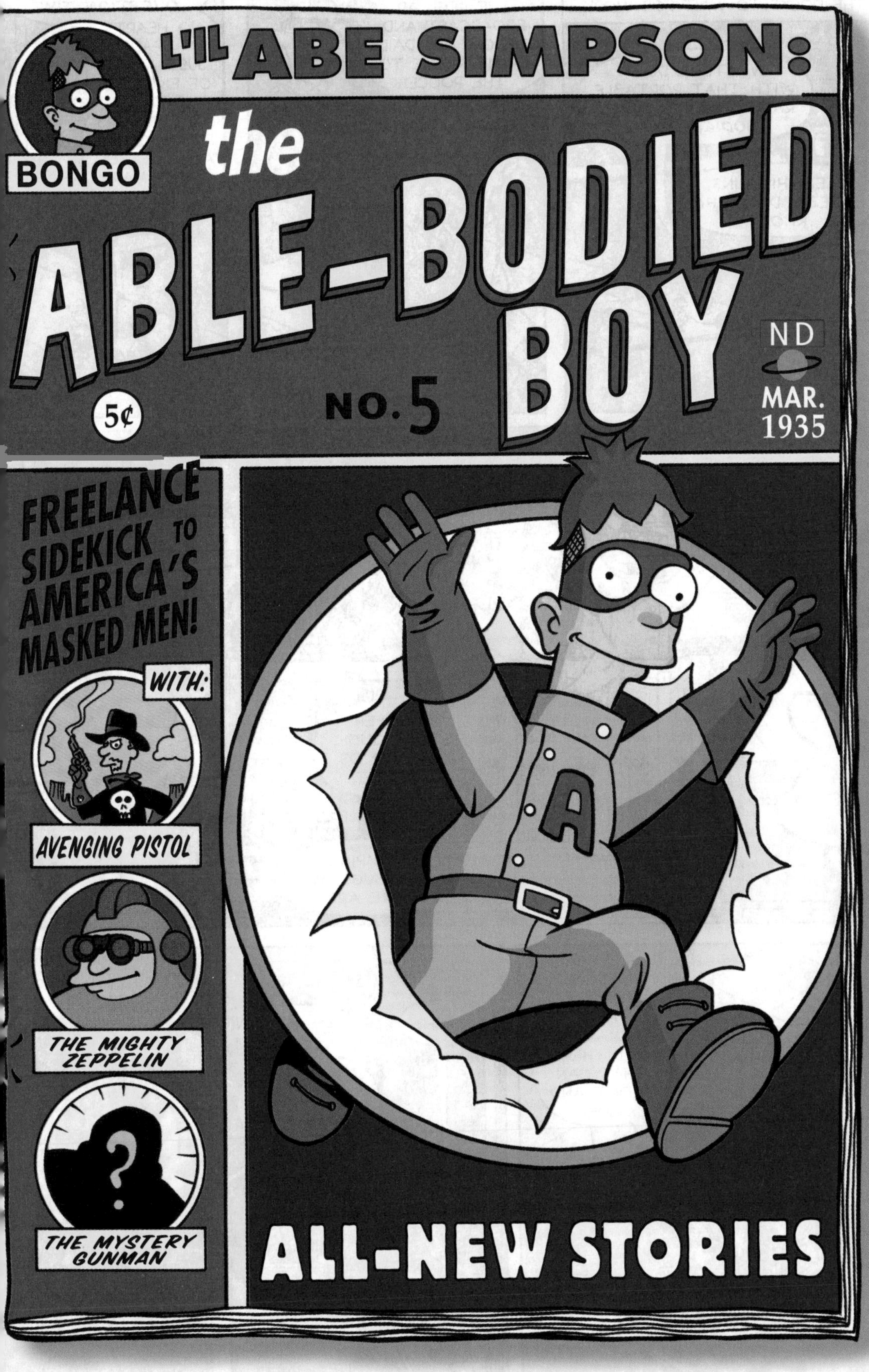
BONGO
L'IL ABE SIMPSON:
the ABLE-BODIED BOY
5¢
NO. 5
ND
MAR. 1935
FREELANCE SIDEKICK TO AMERICA'S MASKED MEN!
WITH:
AVENGING PISTOL
A
THE MIGHTY ZEPPELIN
?
THE MYSTERY GUNMAN
ALL-NEW STORIES

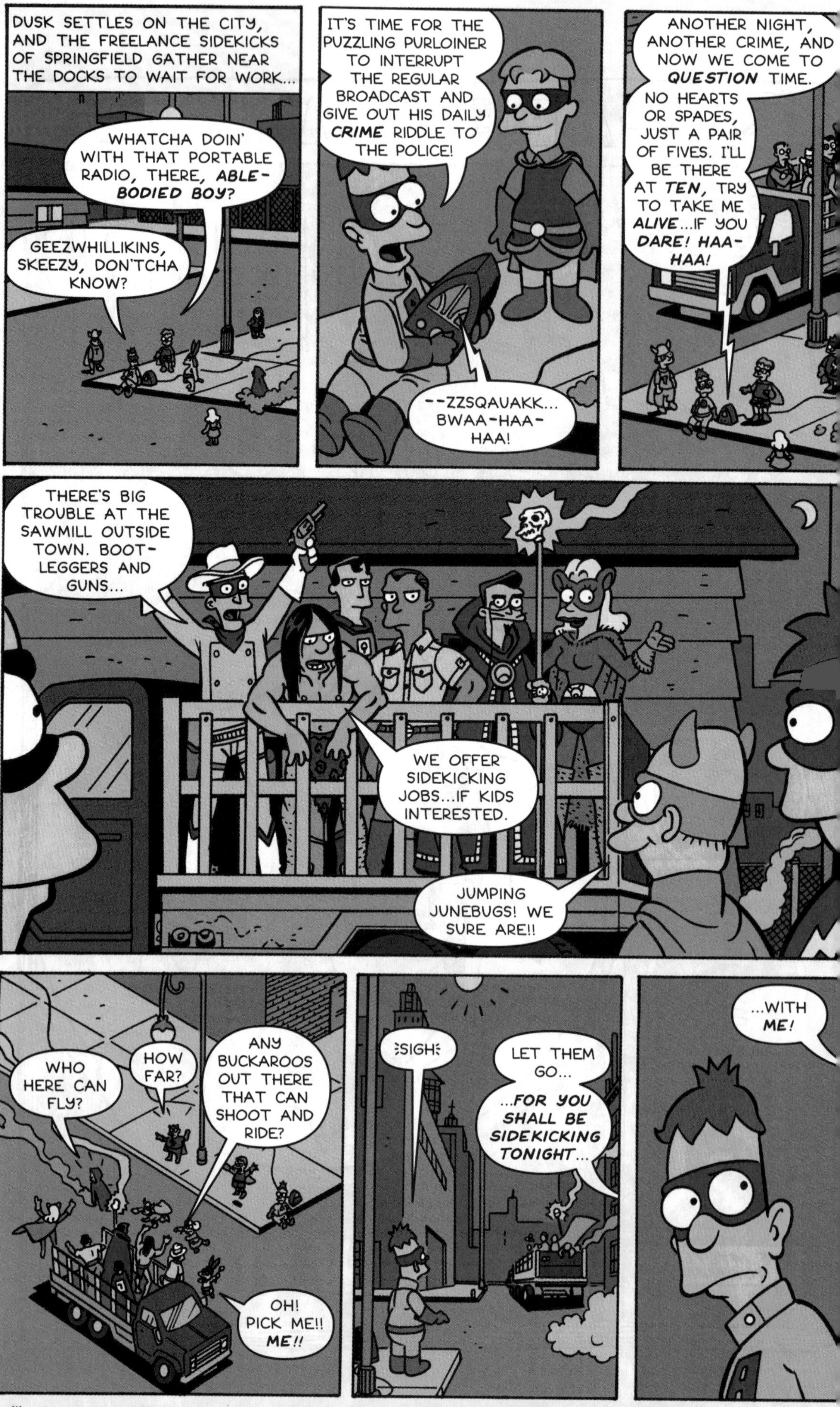
DUSK SETTLES ON THE CITY, AND THE FREELANCE SIDEKICKS OF SPRINGFIELD GATHER NEAR THE DOCKS TO WAIT FOR WORK...
WHATCHA DOIN' WITH THAT PORTABLE RADIO, THERE, ABLE-BODIED BOY?
GEEZWHILLIKINS, SKEEZY, DON'TCHA KNOW?
IT'S TIME FOR THE PUZZLING PURLOINER TO INTERRUPT THE REGULAR BROADCAST AND GIVE OUT HIS DAILY CRIME RIDDLE TO THE POLICE!
--ZZSQAUAKK... BWAA-HAA-HAA!
ANOTHER NIGHT, ANOTHER CRIME, AND NOW WE COME TO QUESTION TIME.
NO HEARTS OR SPADES, JUST A PAIR OF FIVES. I'LL BE THERE AT TEN, TRY TO TAKE ME ALIVE...IF YOU DARE! HAA-HAA!
THERE'S BIG TROUBLE AT THE SAWMILL OUTSIDE TOWN. BOOT-LEGGERS AND GUNS...
WE OFFER SIDEKICKING JOBS...IF KIDS INTERESTED.
JUMPING JUNEBUGS! WE SURE ARE!!
WHO HERE CAN FLY?
HOW FAR?
ANY BUCKAROOS OUT THERE THAT CAN SHOOT AND RIDE?
OH! PICK ME!! ME!!
SIGH
LET THEM GO...
...FOR YOU SHALL BE SIDEKICKING TONIGHT...
...WITH ME!

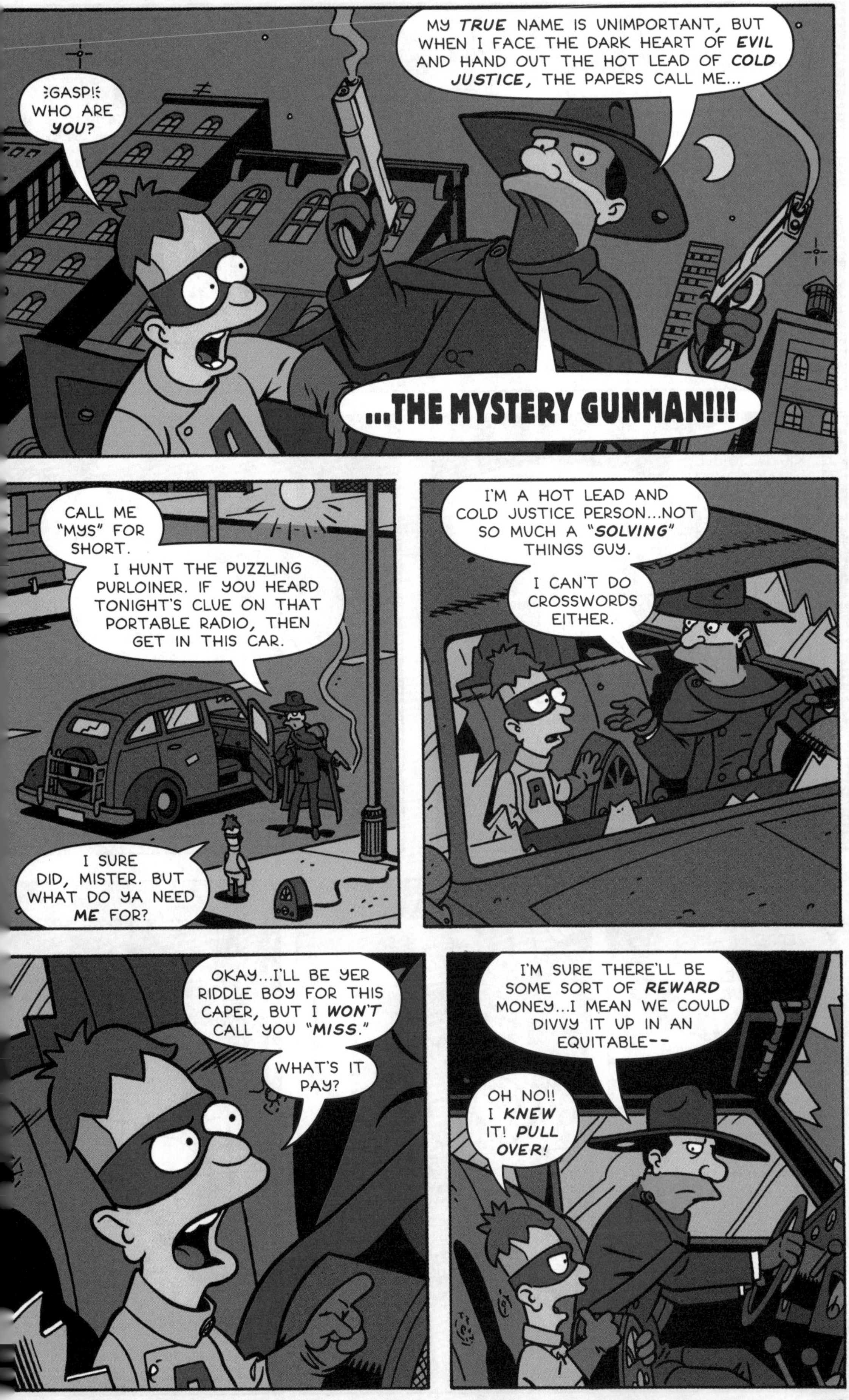

¡GASP!¡ WHO ARE YOU?
MY TRUE NAME IS UNIMPORTANT, BUT WHEN I FACE THE DARK HEART OF EVIL AND HAND OUT THE HOT LEAD OF COLD JUSTICE, THE PAPERS CALL ME...
...THE MYSTERY GUNMAN!!!
CALL ME "MYS" FOR SHORT.
I HUNT THE PUZZLING PURLOINER. IF YOU HEARD TONIGHT'S CLUE ON THAT PORTABLE RADIO, THEN GET IN THIS CAR.
I SURE DID, MISTER. BUT WHAT DO YA NEED ME FOR?
I'M A HOT LEAD AND COLD JUSTICE PERSON...NOT SO MUCH A "SOLVING" THINGS GUY.
I CAN'T DO CROSSWORDS EITHER.
OKAY...I'LL BE YER RIDDLE BOY FOR THIS CAPER, BUT I WON'T CALL YOU "MISS."
WHAT'S IT PAY?
I'M SURE THERE'LL BE SOME SORT OF REWARD MONEY...I MEAN WE COULD DIVVY IT UP IN AN EQUITABLE--
OH NO!! I KNEW IT! PULL OVER!

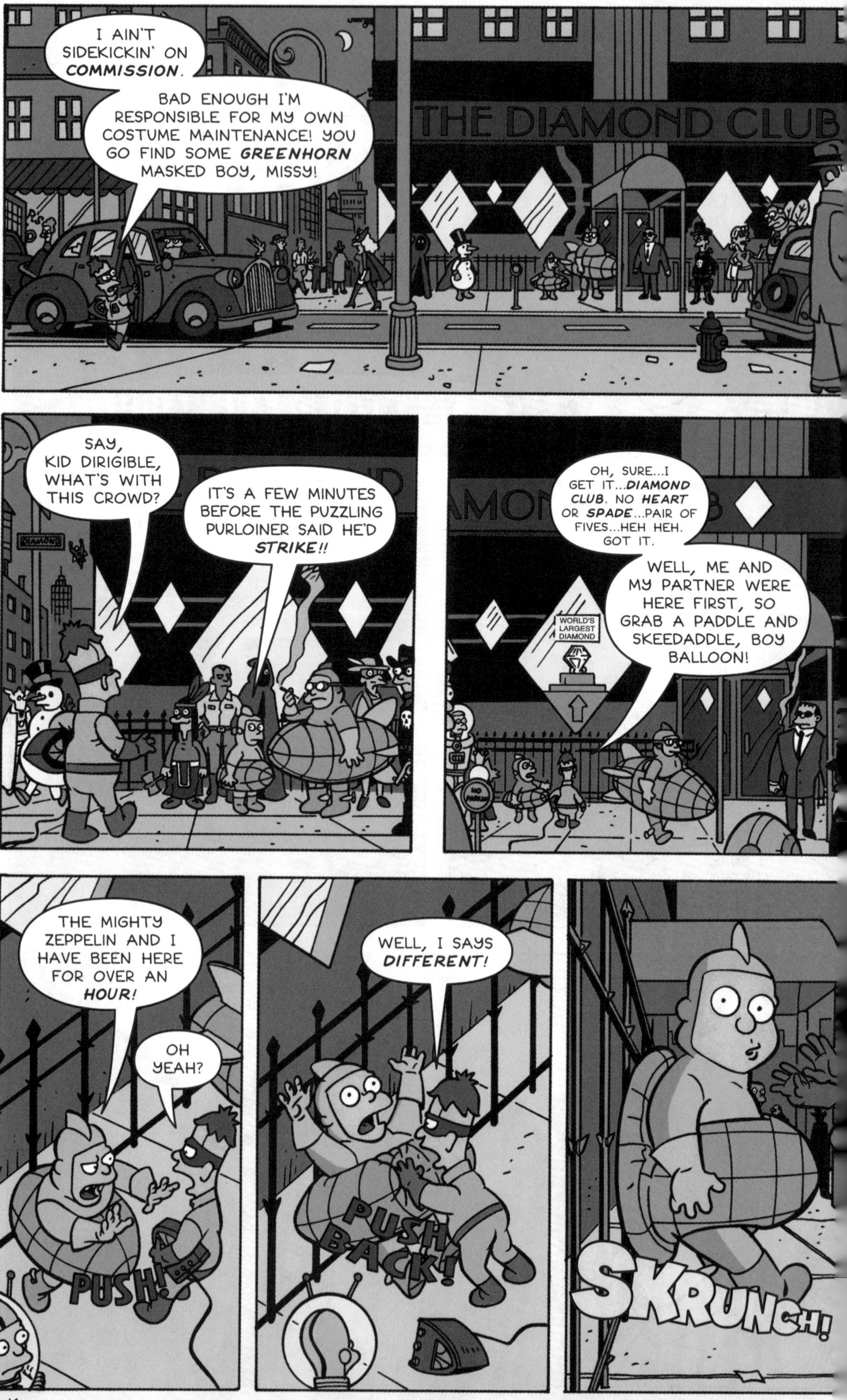
I AIN'T SIDEKICKIN' ON COMMISSION.
BAD ENOUGH I'M RESPONSIBLE FOR MY OWN COSTUME MAINTENANCE! YOU GO FIND SOME GREENHORN MASKED BOY, MISSY!
THE DIAMOND CLUB
SAY, KID DIRIGIBLE, WHAT'S WITH THIS CROWD?
IT'S A FEW MINUTES BEFORE THE PUZZLING PURLOINER SAID HE'D STRIKE!!
OH, SURE...I GET IT...DIAMOND CLUB. NO HEART OR SPADE...PAIR OF FIVES...HEH HEH. GOT IT.
WORLD'S LARGEST DIAMOND
WELL, ME AND MY PARTNER WERE HERE FIRST, SO GRAB A PADDLE AND SKEEDADDLE, BOY BALLOON!
THE MIGHTY ZEPPELIN AND I HAVE BEEN HERE FOR OVER AN HOUR!
OH YEAH?
PUSH!
WELL, I SAYS DIFFERENT!
PUSH BACK!
SKRUNCH!

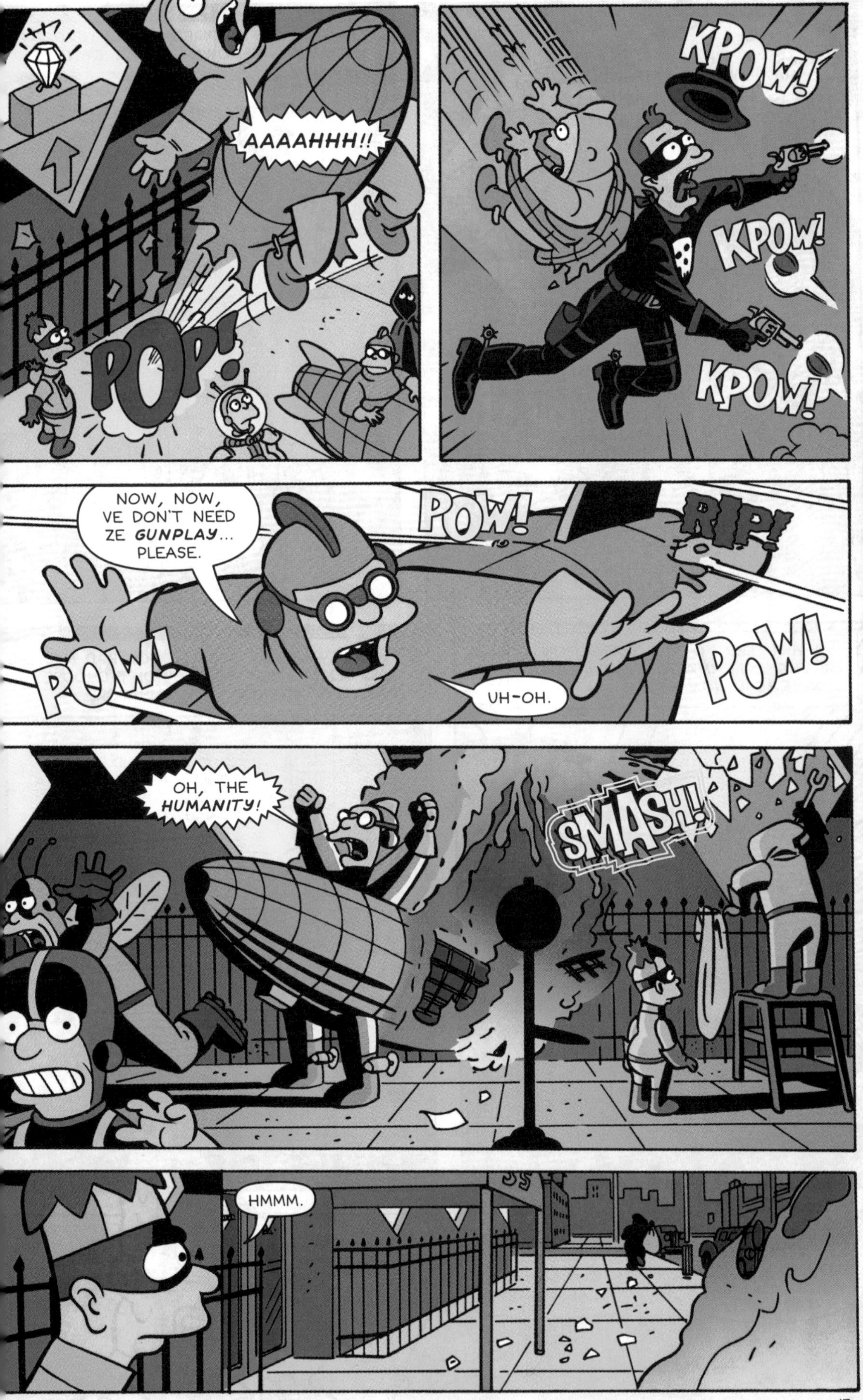
AAAAHHH!!
POP!
KPOW!
KPOW!
KPOW!
NOW, NOW, VE DON'T NEED ZE GUNPLAY... PLEASE.
POW!
RIP!
POW!
POW!
UH-OH.
OH, THE HUMANITY!
SMASH!
HMMM.

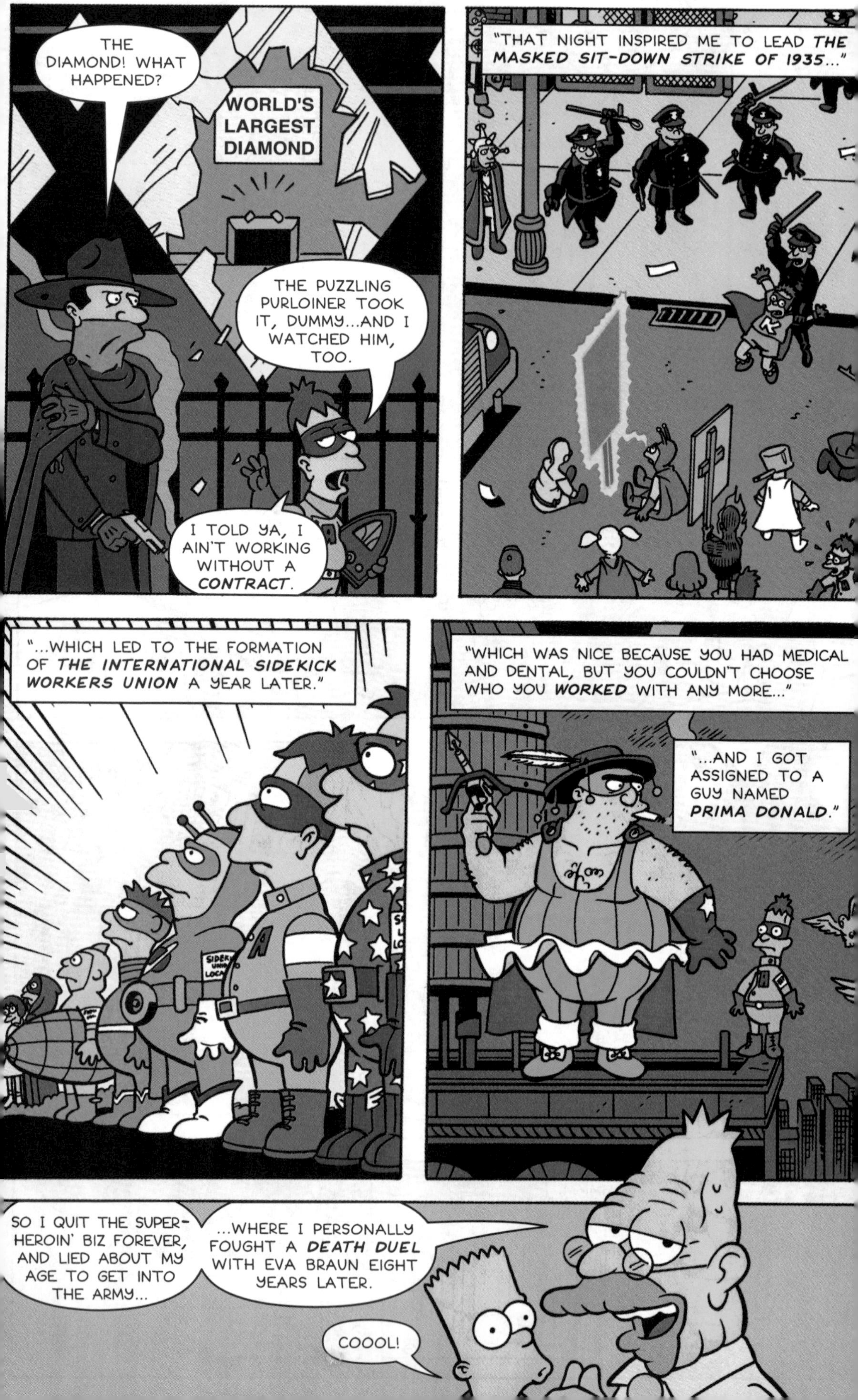
THE DIAMOND! WHAT HAPPENED?
WORLD'S LARGEST DIAMOND
THE PUZZLING PURLOINER TOOK IT, DUMMY...AND I WATCHED HIM, TOO.
I TOLD YA, I AIN'T WORKING WITHOUT A CONTRACT.
"THAT NIGHT INSPIRED ME TO LEAD THE MASKED SIT-DOWN STRIKE OF 1935..."
"...WHICH LED TO THE FORMATION OF THE INTERNATIONAL SIDEKICK WORKERS UNION A YEAR LATER."
"WHICH WAS NICE BECAUSE YOU HAD MEDICAL AND DENTAL, BUT YOU COULDN'T CHOOSE WHO YOU WORKED WITH ANY MORE..."
"...AND I GOT ASSIGNED TO A GUY NAMED PRIMA DONALD."
SO I QUIT THE SUPER-HEROIN' BIZ FOREVER, AND LIED ABOUT MY AGE TO GET INTO THE ARMY...
...WHERE I PERSONALLY FOUGHT A DEATH DUEL WITH EVA BRAUN EIGHT YEARS LATER.
COOOL!

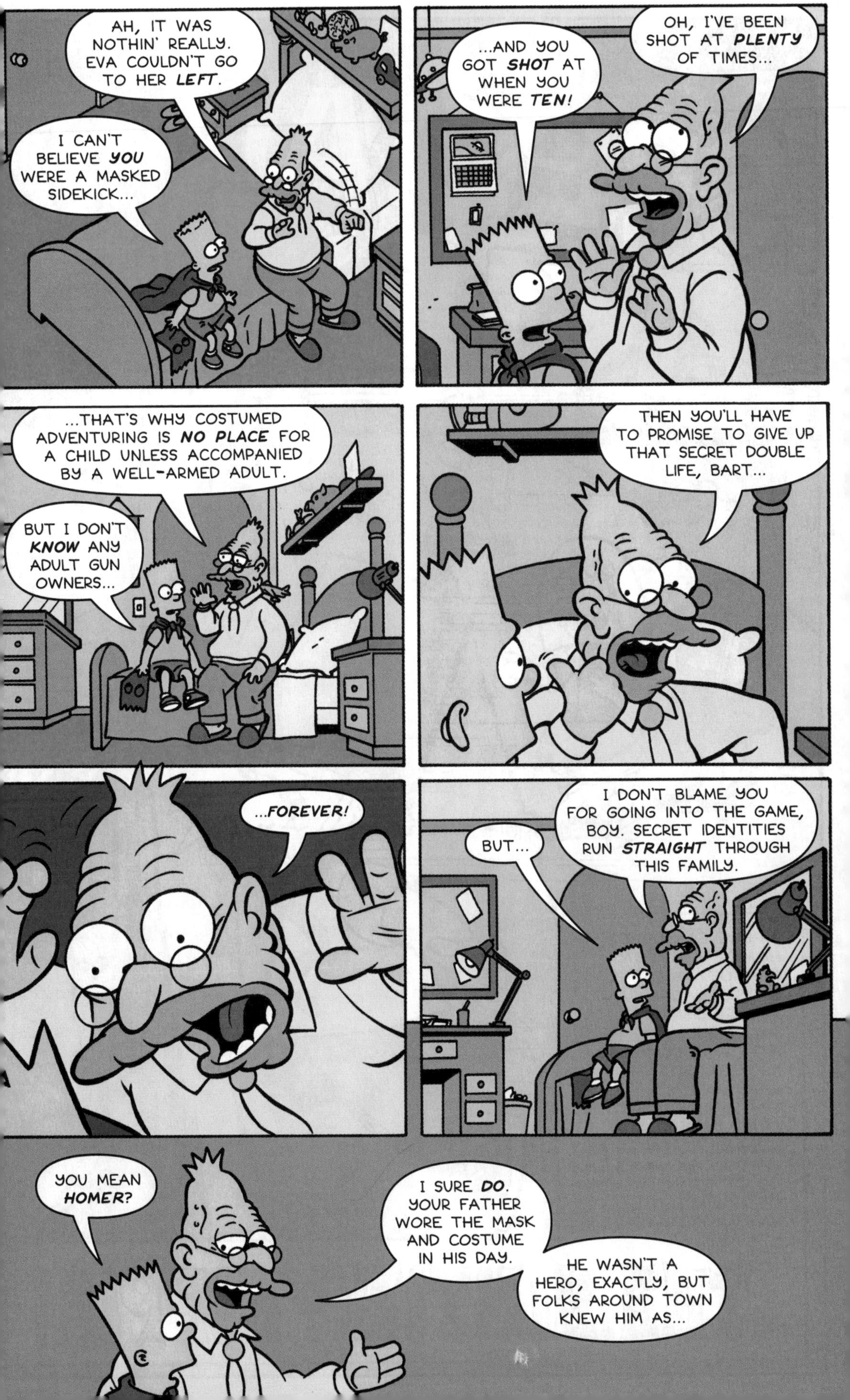
AH, IT WAS NOTHIN' REALLY. EVA COULDN'T GO TO HER *LEFT*.
I CAN'T BELIEVE *YOU* WERE A MASKED SIDEKICK...
...AND YOU GOT *SHOT* AT WHEN YOU WERE *TEN*!
OH, I'VE BEEN SHOT AT *PLENTY* OF TIMES...
...THAT'S WHY COSTUMED ADVENTURING IS *NO PLACE* FOR A CHILD UNLESS ACCOMPANIED BY A WELL-ARMED ADULT.
BUT I DON'T *KNOW* ANY ADULT GUN OWNERS...
THEN YOU'LL HAVE TO PROMISE TO GIVE UP THAT SECRET DOUBLE LIFE, BART...
...*FOREVER*!
I DON'T BLAME YOU FOR GOING INTO THE GAME, BOY. SECRET IDENTITIES RUN *STRAIGHT* THROUGH THIS FAMILY.
BUT...
YOU MEAN *HOMER*?
I SURE *DO*. YOUR FATHER WORE THE MASK AND COSTUME IN HIS DAY.
HE WASN'T A HERO, EXACTLY, BUT FOLKS AROUND TOWN KNEW HIM AS...

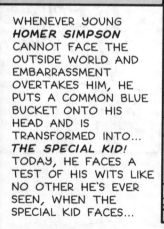

THE SPECIAL KID

D'OH!

WHENEVER YOUNG **HOMER SIMPSON** CANNOT FACE THE OUTSIDE WORLD AND EMBARRASSMENT OVERTAKES HIM, HE PUTS A COMMON BLUE BUCKET ONTO HIS HEAD AND IS TRANSFORMED INTO... **THE SPECIAL KID!** TODAY, HE FACES A TEST OF HIS WITS LIKE NO OTHER HE'S EVER SEEN, WHEN THE SPECIAL KID FACES...

...THE HUNTING HIPPIE!

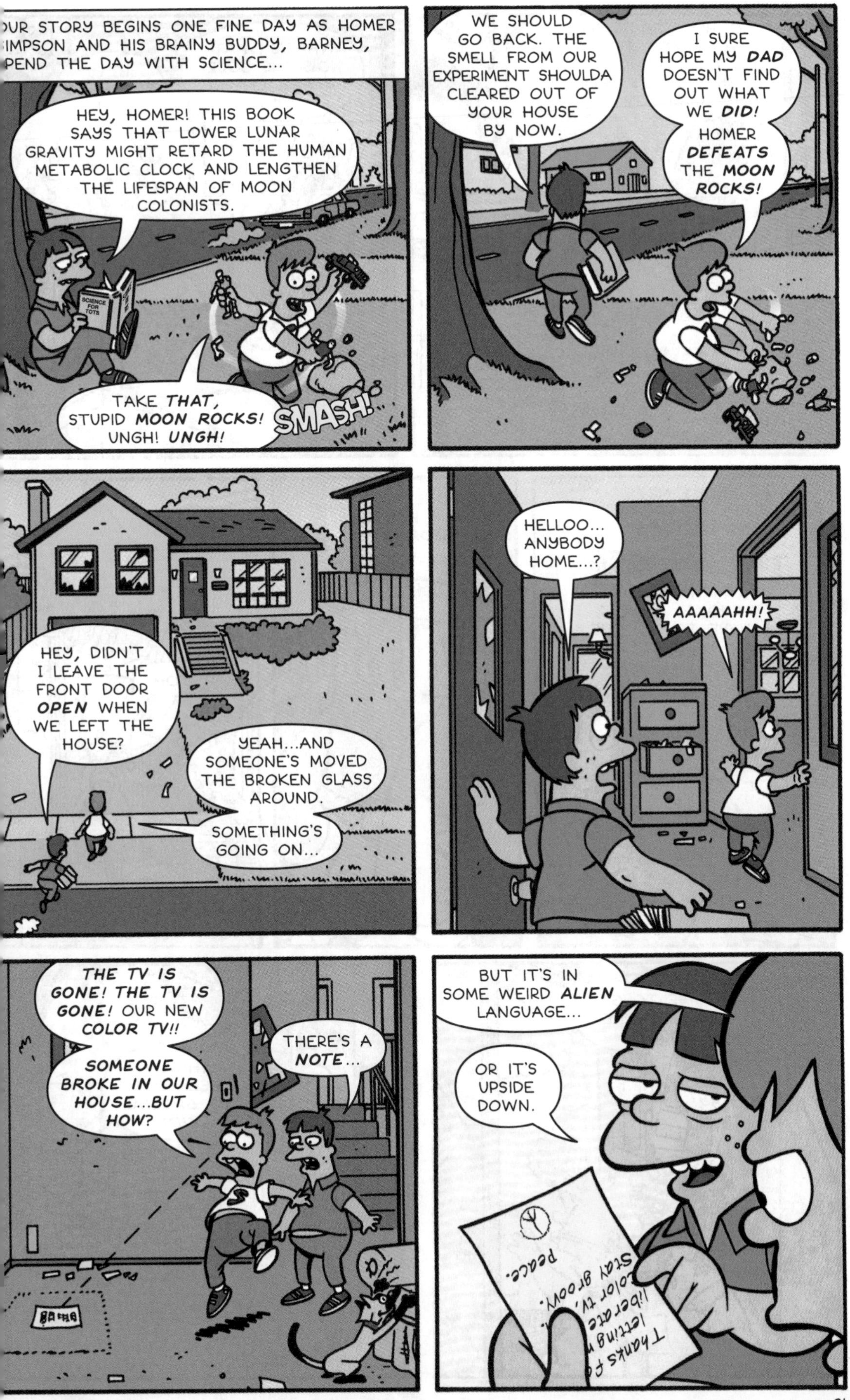

UR STORY BEGINS ONE FINE DAY AS HOMER IMPSON AND HIS BRAINY BUDDY, BARNEY, PEND THE DAY WITH SCIENCE...
HEY, HOMER! THIS BOOK SAYS THAT LOWER LUNAR GRAVITY MIGHT RETARD THE HUMAN METABOLIC CLOCK AND LENGTHEN THE LIFESPAN OF MOON COLONISTS.
SCIENCE FOR TOTS
TAKE THAT, STUPID MOON ROCKS! UNGH! UNGH!
SMASH!
WE SHOULD GO BACK. THE SMELL FROM OUR EXPERIMENT SHOULDA CLEARED OUT OF YOUR HOUSE BY NOW.
I SURE HOPE MY DAD DOESN'T FIND OUT WHAT WE DID!
HOMER DEFEATS THE MOON ROCKS!
HEY, DIDN'T I LEAVE THE FRONT DOOR OPEN WHEN WE LEFT THE HOUSE?
YEAH...AND SOMEONE'S MOVED THE BROKEN GLASS AROUND.
SOMETHING'S GOING ON...
HELLOO... ANYBODY HOME...?
AAAAAHH!
THE TV IS GONE! THE TV IS GONE! OUR NEW COLOR TV!!
SOMEONE BROKE IN OUR HOUSE...BUT HOW?
THERE'S A NOTE...
BUT IT'S IN SOME WEIRD ALIEN LANGUAGE...
OR IT'S UPSIDE DOWN.
color tv,
Stay groovy.
peace.

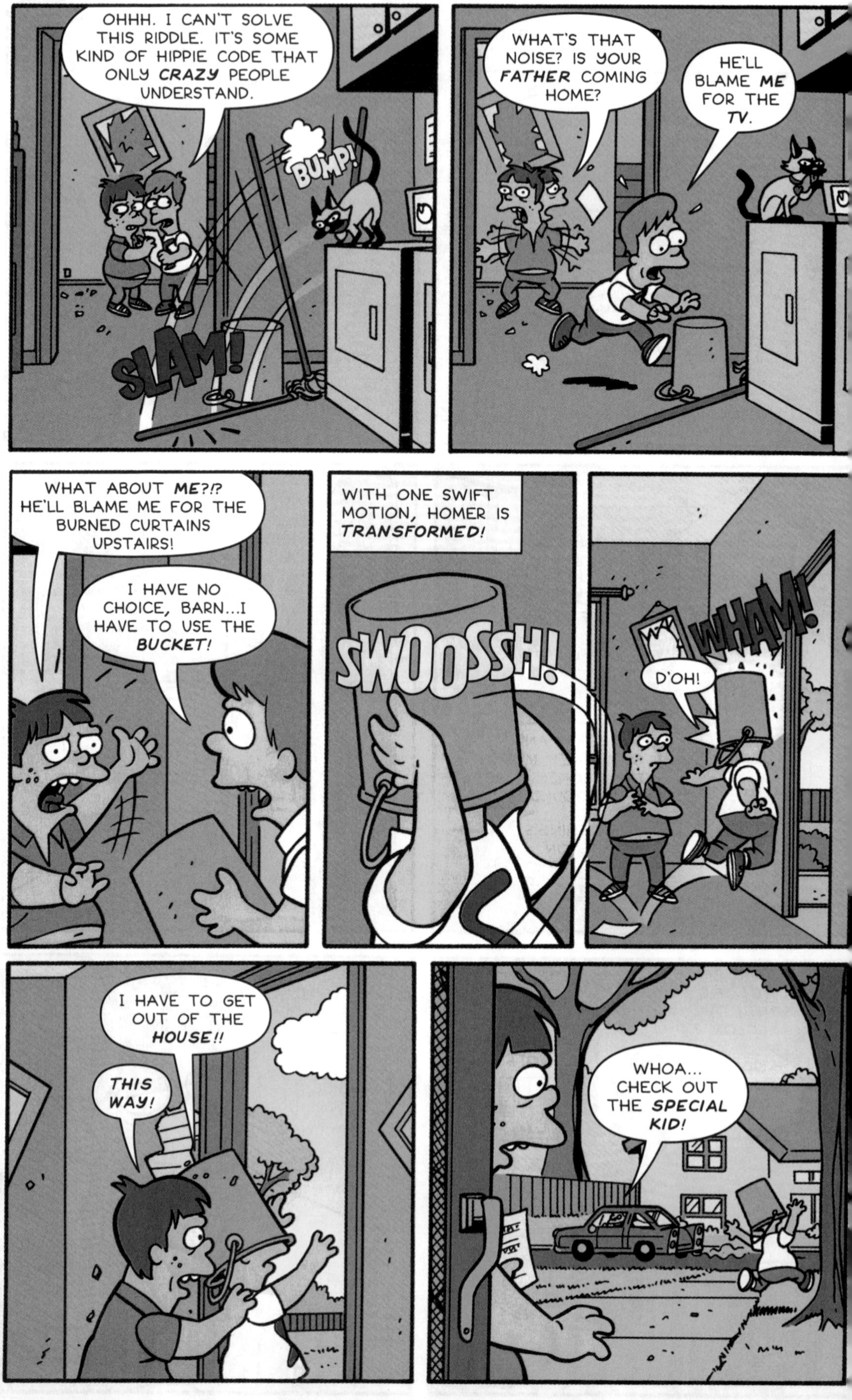
OHHH. I CAN'T SOLVE THIS RIDDLE. IT'S SOME KIND OF HIPPIE CODE THAT ONLY CRAZY PEOPLE UNDERSTAND.
BUMP!
SLAM!
WHAT'S THAT NOISE? IS YOUR FATHER COMING HOME?
HE'LL BLAME ME FOR THE TV.
WHAT ABOUT ME?!? HE'LL BLAME ME FOR THE BURNED CURTAINS UPSTAIRS!
I HAVE NO CHOICE, BARN...I HAVE TO USE THE BUCKET!
WITH ONE SWIFT MOTION, HOMER IS TRANSFORMED!
SWOOSSH!
WHAM!
D'OH!
I HAVE TO GET OUT OF THE HOUSE!!
THIS WAY!
WHOA... CHECK OUT THE SPECIAL KID!

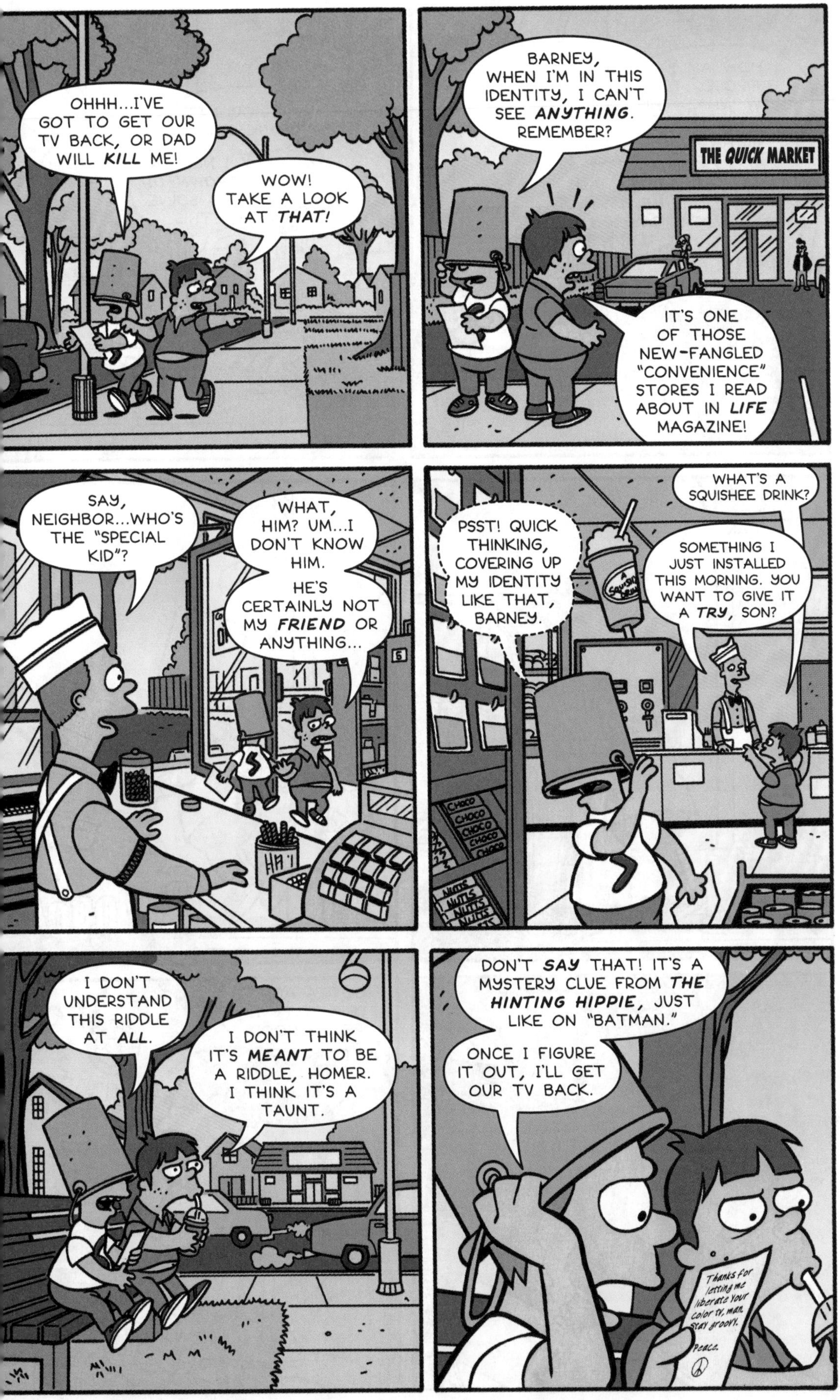
OHHH...I'VE GOT TO GET OUR TV BACK, OR DAD WILL KILL ME!
WOW! TAKE A LOOK AT THAT!
BARNEY, WHEN I'M IN THIS IDENTITY, I CAN'T SEE ANYTHING. REMEMBER?
THE QUICK MARKET
IT'S ONE OF THOSE NEW-FANGLED "CONVENIENCE" STORES I READ ABOUT IN LIFE MAGAZINE!
SAY, NEIGHBOR...WHO'S THE "SPECIAL KID"?
WHAT, HIM? UM...I DON'T KNOW HIM.
HE'S CERTAINLY NOT MY FRIEND OR ANYTHING...
WHAT'S A SQUISHEE DRINK?
PSST! QUICK THINKING, COVERING UP MY IDENTITY LIKE THAT, BARNEY.
SOMETHING I JUST INSTALLED THIS MORNING. YOU WANT TO GIVE IT A TRY, SON?
CHOCO
NUTS
I DON'T UNDERSTAND THIS RIDDLE AT ALL.
I DON'T THINK IT'S MEANT TO BE A RIDDLE, HOMER. I THINK IT'S A TAUNT.
DON'T SAY THAT! IT'S A MYSTERY CLUE FROM THE HINTING HIPPIE, JUST LIKE ON "BATMAN."
ONCE I FIGURE IT OUT, I'LL GET OUR TV BACK.
Thanks for letting me liberate your color tv, man. Stay groovy.
Peace.

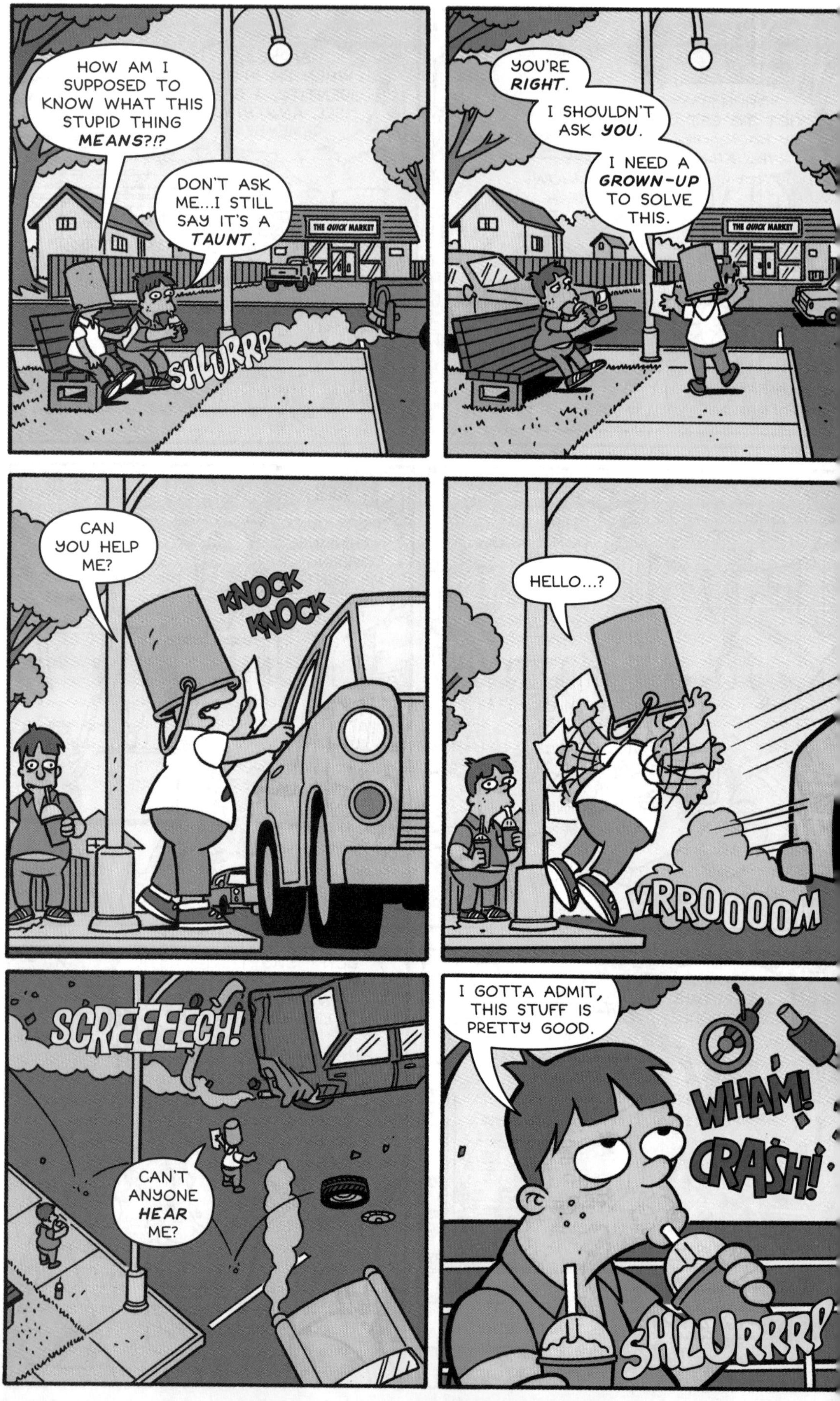
HOW AM I SUPPOSED TO KNOW WHAT THIS STUPID THING MEANS?!?
DON'T ASK ME...I STILL SAY IT'S A TAUNT.
THE QUICK MARKET
SHLURRP
YOU'RE RIGHT.
I SHOULDN'T ASK YOU.
I NEED A GROWN-UP TO SOLVE THIS.
THE QUICK MARKET
CAN YOU HELP ME?
KNOCK KNOCK
HELLO...?
VRROOOOM
SCREEEEECH!
CAN'T ANYONE HEAR ME?
I GOTTA ADMIT, THIS STUFF IS PRETTY GOOD.
WHAM!
CRASH!
SHLURRRP

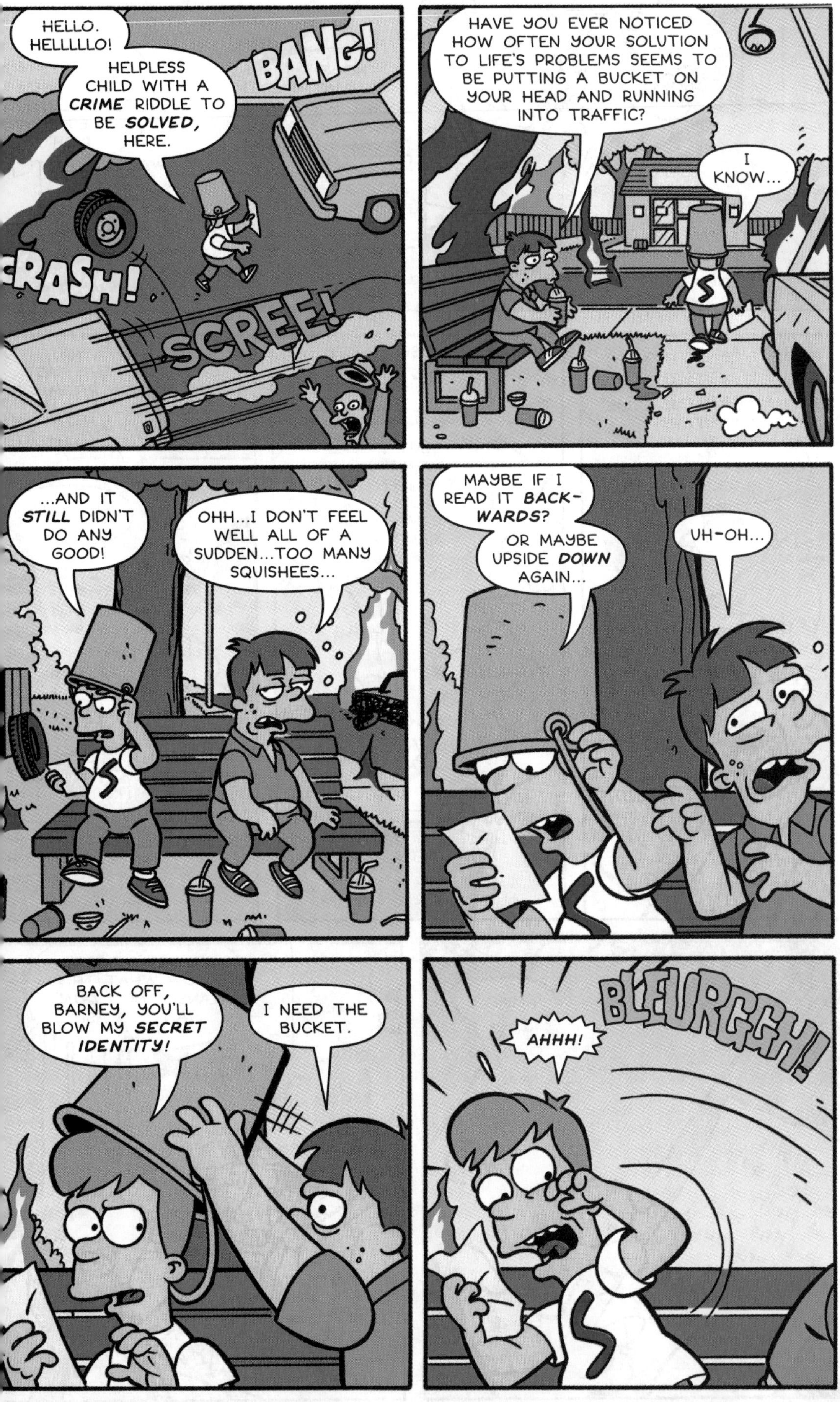
HELLO. HELLLLLO!
HELPLESS CHILD WITH A CRIME RIDDLE TO BE SOLVED, HERE.
BANG!
CRASH!
SCREE!
HAVE YOU EVER NOTICED HOW OFTEN YOUR SOLUTION TO LIFE'S PROBLEMS SEEMS TO BE PUTTING A BUCKET ON YOUR HEAD AND RUNNING INTO TRAFFIC?
I KNOW...
...AND IT STILL DIDN'T DO ANY GOOD!
OHH...I DON'T FEEL WELL ALL OF A SUDDEN...TOO MANY SQUISHEES...
MAYBE IF I READ IT BACK-WARDS?
OR MAYBE UPSIDE DOWN AGAIN...
UH-OH...
BACK OFF, BARNEY, YOU'LL BLOW MY SECRET IDENTITY!
I NEED THE BUCKET.
AHHH!
BLEURGGH!

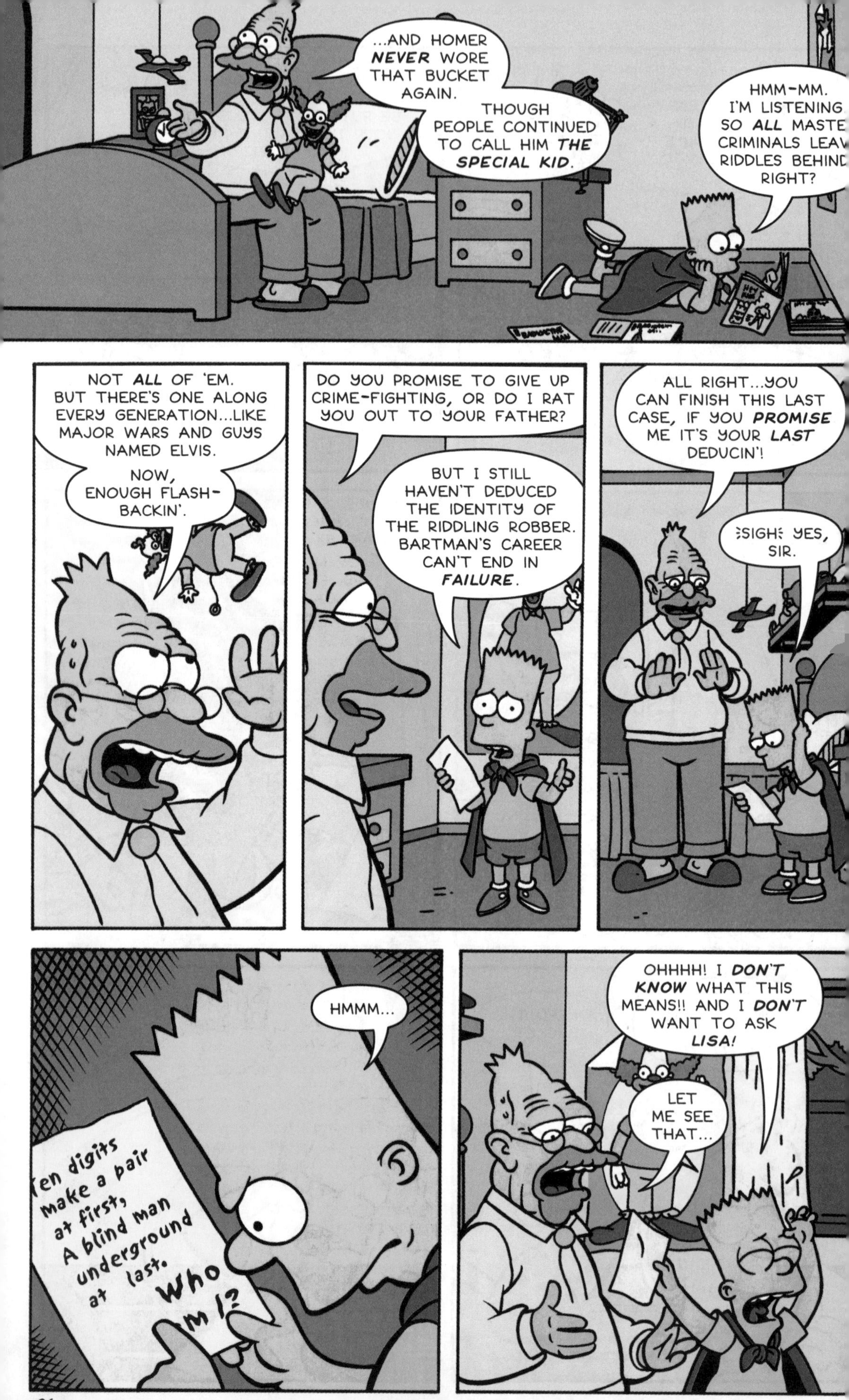
...AND HOMER NEVER WORE THAT BUCKET AGAIN.
THOUGH PEOPLE CONTINUED TO CALL HIM THE SPECIAL KID.
HMM-MM. I'M LISTENING SO ALL MASTE CRIMINALS LEAV RIDDLES BEHIND RIGHT?
NOT ALL OF 'EM. BUT THERE'S ONE ALONG EVERY GENERATION...LIKE MAJOR WARS AND GUYS NAMED ELVIS.
NOW, ENOUGH FLASH-BACKIN'.
DO YOU PROMISE TO GIVE UP CRIME-FIGHTING, OR DO I RAT YOU OUT TO YOUR FATHER?
BUT I STILL HAVEN'T DEDUCED THE IDENTITY OF THE RIDDLING ROBBER. BARTMAN'S CAREER CAN'T END IN FAILURE.
ALL RIGHT...YOU CAN FINISH THIS LAST CASE, IF YOU PROMISE ME IT'S YOUR LAST DEDUCIN'!
:SIGH: YES, SIR.
HMMM...
en digits make a pair at first, A blind man underground at last. Who m I?
OHHHH! I DON'T KNOW WHAT THIS MEANS!! AND I DON'T WANT TO ASK LISA!
LET ME SEE THAT...

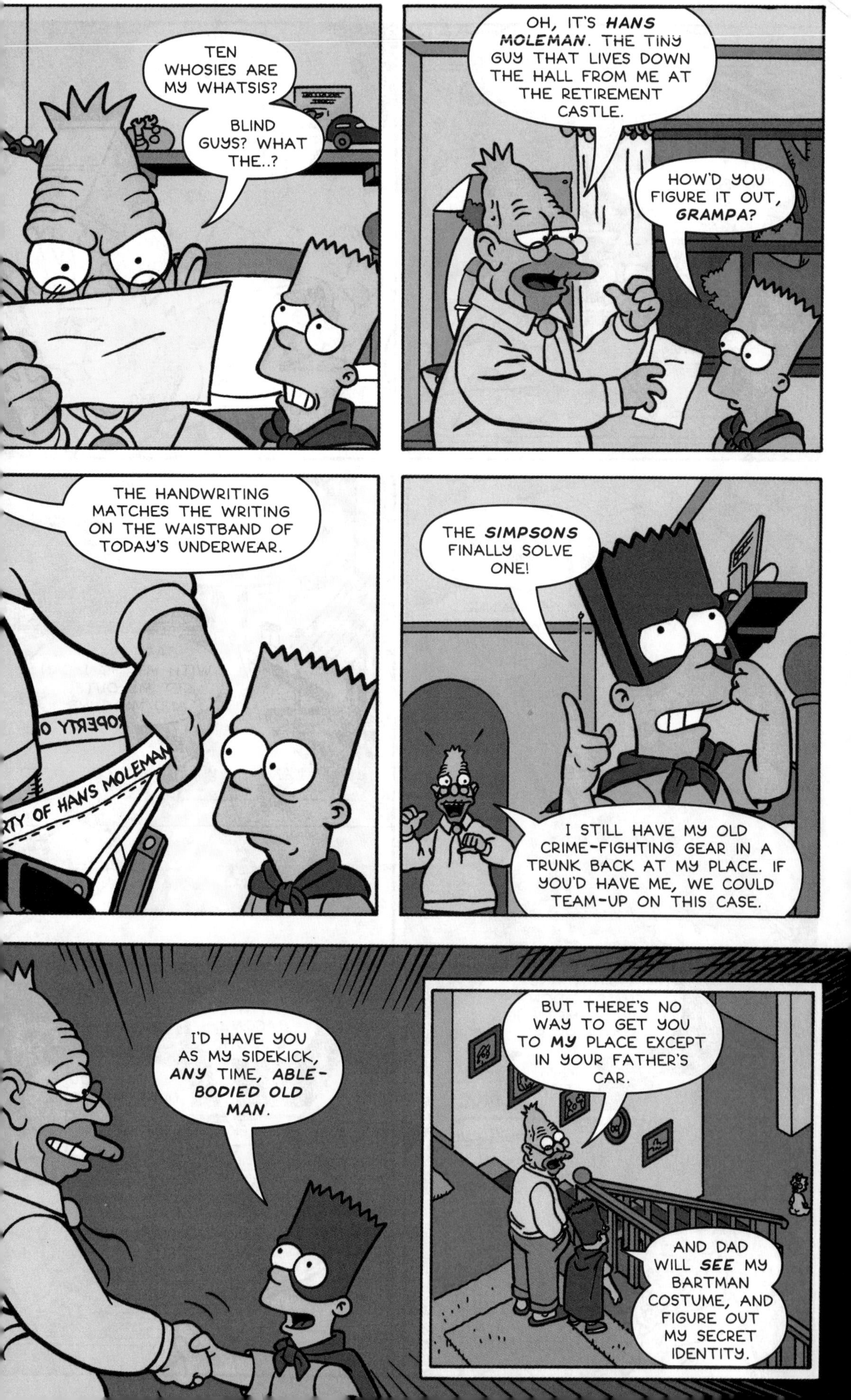
TEN WHOSIES ARE MY WHATSIS?
BLIND GUYS? WHAT THE..?
OH, IT'S **HANS MOLEMAN**. THE TINY GUY THAT LIVES DOWN THE HALL FROM ME AT THE RETIREMENT CASTLE.
HOW'D YOU FIGURE IT OUT, **GRAMPA**?
THE HANDWRITING MATCHES THE WRITING ON THE WAISTBAND OF TODAY'S UNDERWEAR.
ROPERTY OF HANS MOLEMAN
THE **SIMPSONS** FINALLY SOLVE ONE!
I STILL HAVE MY OLD CRIME-FIGHTING GEAR IN A TRUNK BACK AT MY PLACE. IF YOU'D HAVE ME, WE COULD TEAM-UP ON THIS CASE.
I'D HAVE YOU AS MY SIDEKICK, **ANY** TIME, **ABLE-BODIED OLD MAN**.
BUT THERE'S NO WAY TO GET YOU TO **MY** PLACE EXCEPT IN YOUR FATHER'S CAR.
AND DAD WILL **SEE** MY BARTMAN COSTUME, AND FIGURE OUT MY SECRET IDENTITY.

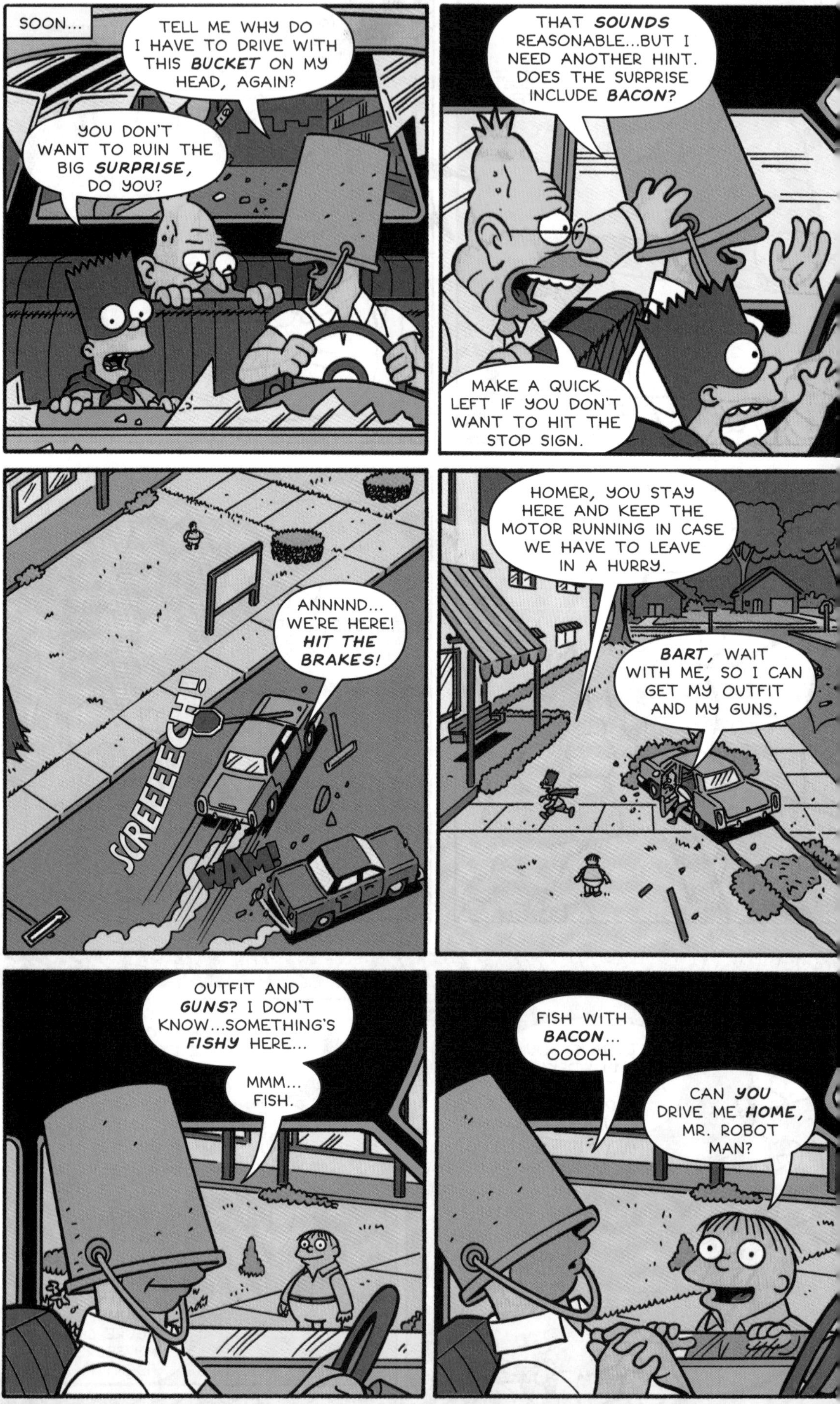
SOON...
TELL ME WHY DO I HAVE TO DRIVE WITH THIS BUCKET ON MY HEAD, AGAIN?
YOU DON'T WANT TO RUIN THE BIG SURPRISE, DO YOU?
THAT SOUNDS REASONABLE...BUT I NEED ANOTHER HINT. DOES THE SURPRISE INCLUDE BACON?
MAKE A QUICK LEFT IF YOU DON'T WANT TO HIT THE STOP SIGN.
ANNNND... WE'RE HERE! HIT THE BRAKES!
SCREEEECH!
WAM!
HOMER, YOU STAY HERE AND KEEP THE MOTOR RUNNING IN CASE WE HAVE TO LEAVE IN A HURRY.
BART, WAIT WITH ME, SO I CAN GET MY OUTFIT AND MY GUNS.
OUTFIT AND GUNS? I DON'T KNOW...SOMETHING'S FISHY HERE...
MMM... FISH.
FISH WITH BACON... OOOOH.
CAN YOU DRIVE ME HOME, MR. ROBOT MAN?

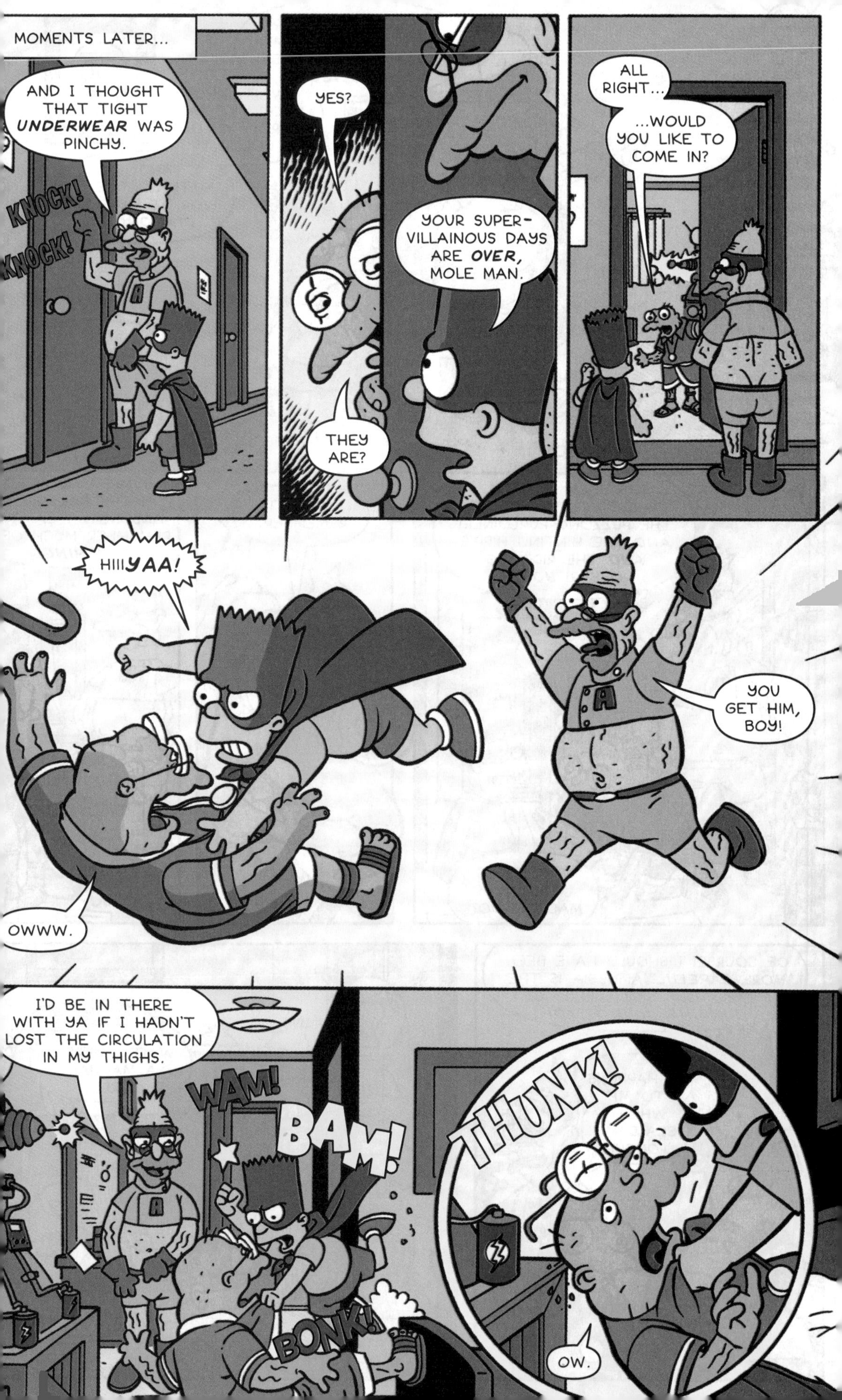
MOMENTS LATER...
AND I THOUGHT THAT TIGHT UNDERWEAR WAS PINCHY.
KNOCK! KNOCK!
YES?
YOUR SUPER-VILLAINOUS DAYS ARE OVER, MOLE MAN.
THEY ARE?
ALL RIGHT...
...WOULD YOU LIKE TO COME IN?
HIIIYAA!
YOU GET HIM, BOY!
OWWW.
I'D BE IN THERE WITH YA IF I HADN'T LOST THE CIRCULATION IN MY THIGHS.
WAM!
BAM!
BONK!
THUNK!
OW.

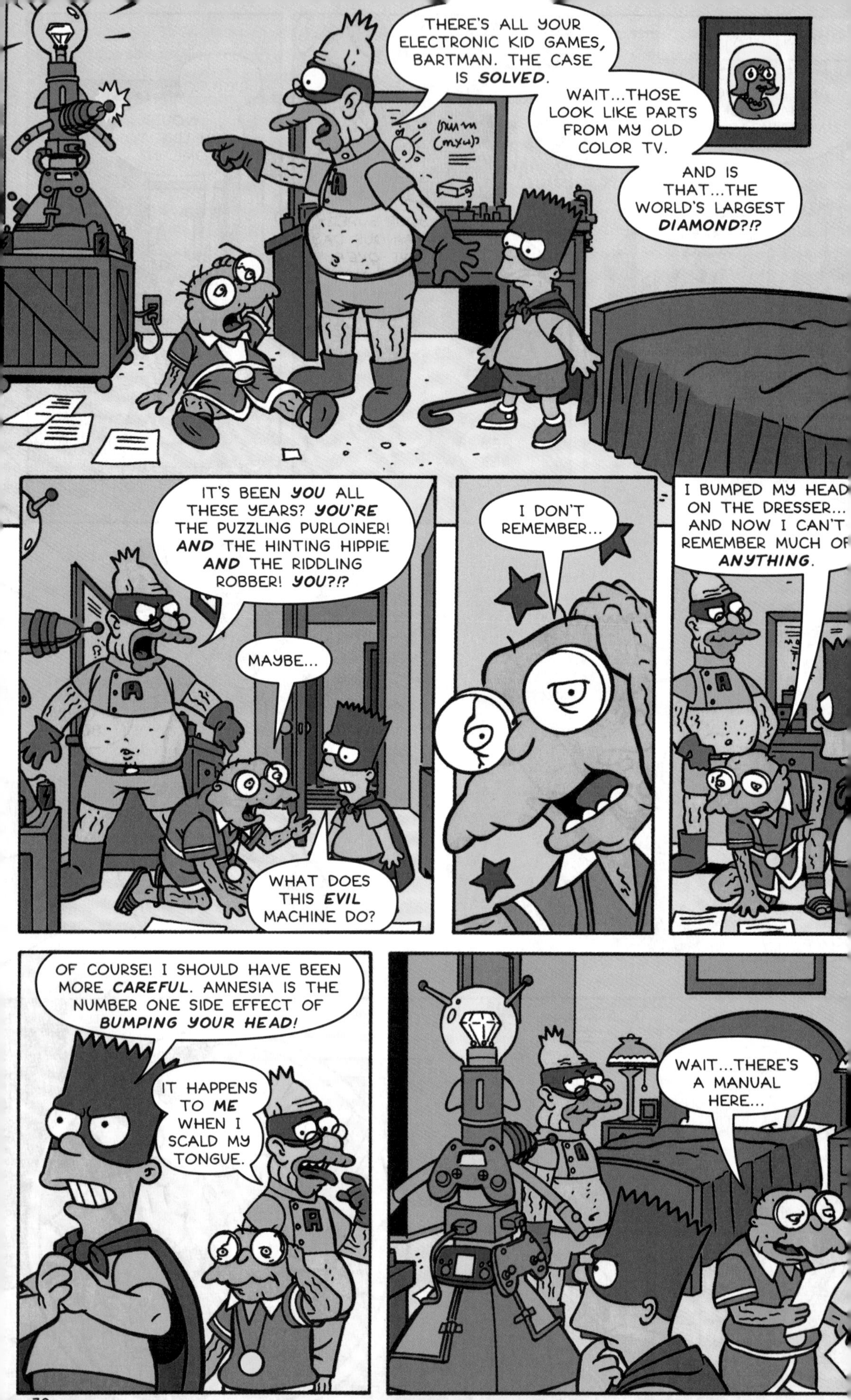
THERE'S ALL YOUR ELECTRONIC KID GAMES, BARTMAN. THE CASE IS SOLVED.
WAIT...THOSE LOOK LIKE PARTS FROM MY OLD COLOR TV.
AND IS THAT...THE WORLD'S LARGEST DIAMOND?!?
IT'S BEEN YOU ALL THESE YEARS? YOU'RE THE PUZZLING PURLOINER! AND THE HINTING HIPPIE AND THE RIDDLING ROBBER! YOU?!?
MAYBE...
WHAT DOES THIS EVIL MACHINE DO?
I DON'T REMEMBER...
I BUMPED MY HEAD ON THE DRESSER... AND NOW I CAN'T REMEMBER MUCH OF ANYTHING.
OF COURSE! I SHOULD HAVE BEEN MORE CAREFUL. AMNESIA IS THE NUMBER ONE SIDE EFFECT OF BUMPING YOUR HEAD!
IT HAPPENS TO ME WHEN I SCALD MY TONGUE.
WAIT...THERE'S A MANUAL HERE...

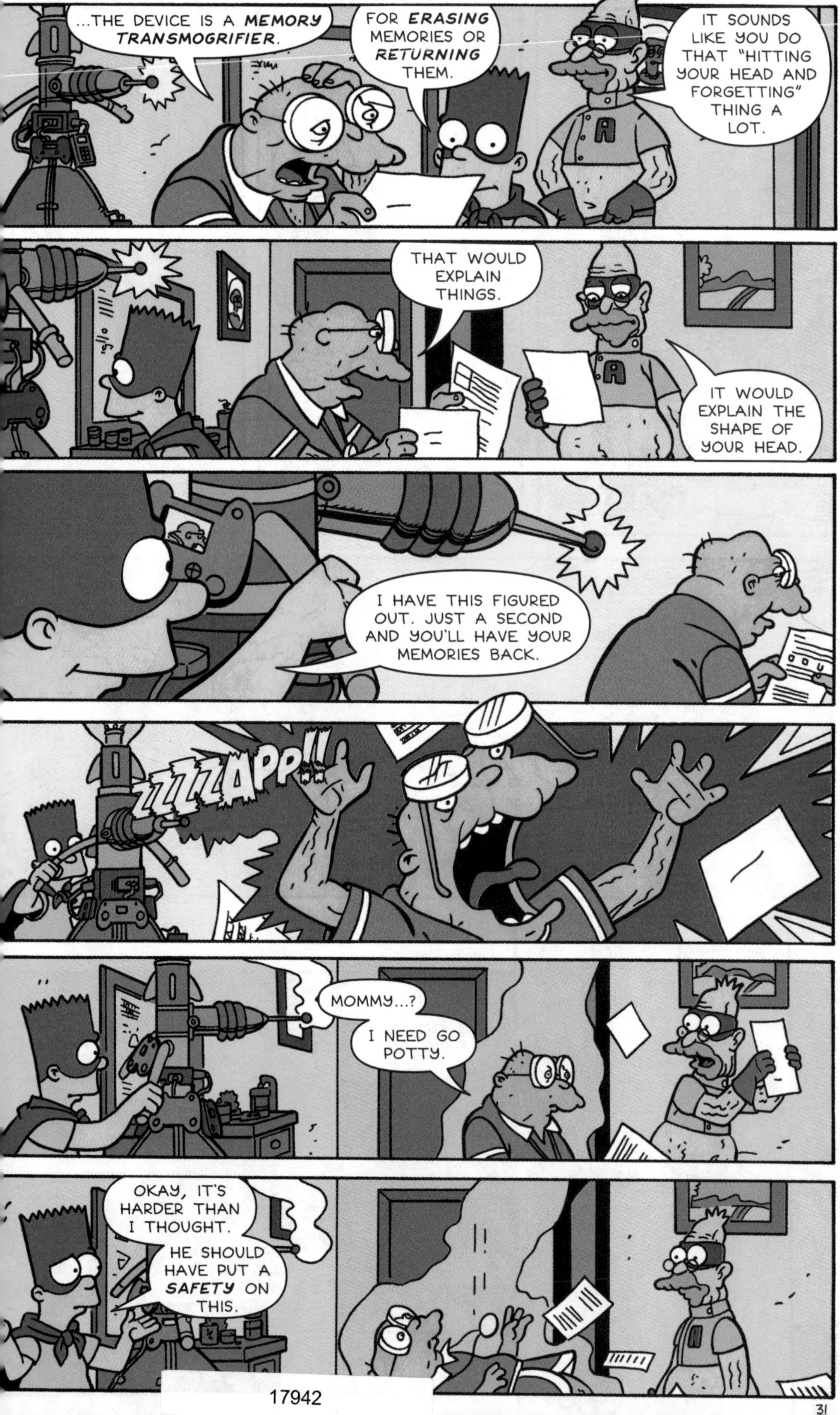
...THE DEVICE IS A MEMORY TRANSMOGRIFIER.
FOR ERASING MEMORIES OR RETURNING THEM.
IT SOUNDS LIKE YOU DO THAT "HITTING YOUR HEAD AND FORGETTING" THING A LOT.
THAT WOULD EXPLAIN THINGS.
IT WOULD EXPLAIN THE SHAPE OF YOUR HEAD.
I HAVE THIS FIGURED OUT. JUST A SECOND AND YOU'LL HAVE YOUR MEMORIES BACK.
ZZZZZAPP!!
MOMMY...?
I NEED GO POTTY.
OKAY, IT'S HARDER THAN I THOUGHT.
HE SHOULD HAVE PUT A SAFETY ON THIS.

17942

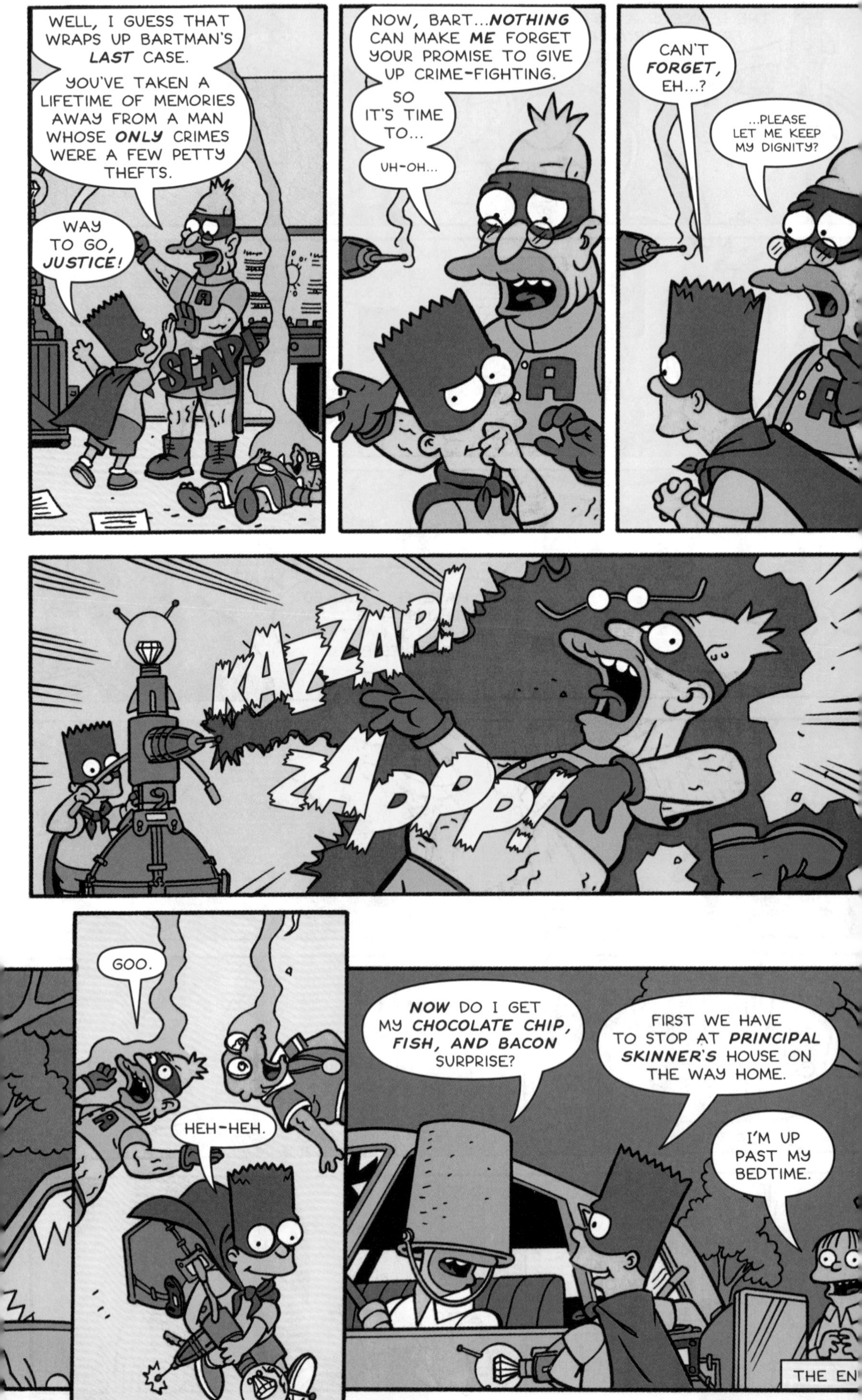
WELL, I GUESS THAT WRAPS UP BARTMAN'S LAST CASE.
YOU'VE TAKEN A LIFETIME OF MEMORIES AWAY FROM A MAN WHOSE ONLY CRIMES WERE A FEW PETTY THEFTS.
WAY TO GO, JUSTICE!
SLAP!
NOW, BART...NOTHING CAN MAKE ME FORGET YOUR PROMISE TO GIVE UP CRIME-FIGHTING.
SO IT'S TIME TO...
UH-OH...
CAN'T FORGET, EH...?
...PLEASE LET ME KEEP MY DIGNITY?
KAZZAP!
ZAPPP!
GOO.
HEH-HEH.
NOW DO I GET MY CHOCOLATE CHIP, FISH, AND BACON SURPRISE?
FIRST WE HAVE TO STOP AT PRINCIPAL SKINNER'S HOUSE ON THE WAY HOME.
I'M UP PAST MY BEDTIME.
THE EN

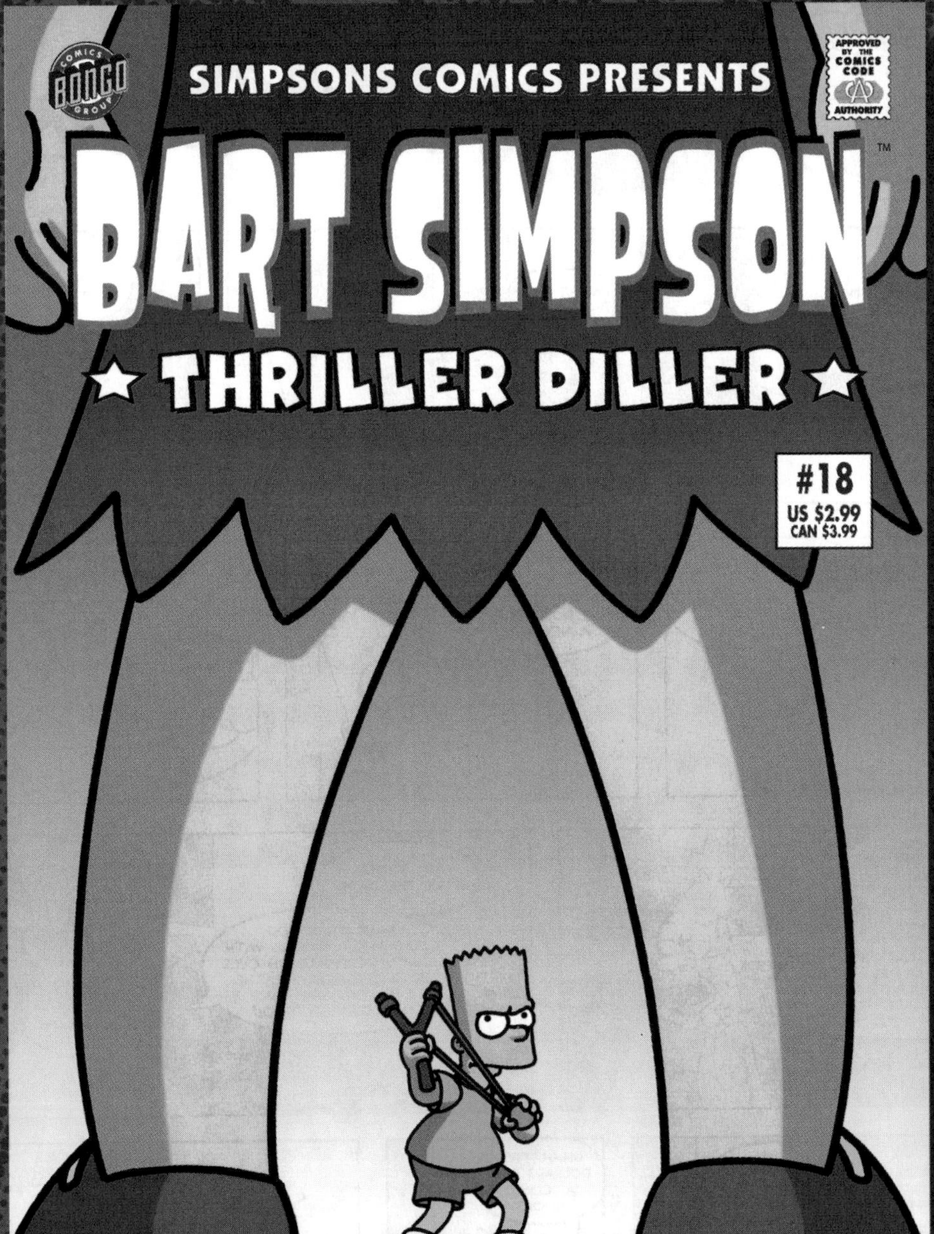
SIMPSONS COMICS PRESENTS
BART SIMPSON
THRILLER DILLER
#18
US $2.99
CAN $3.99
APPROVED BY THE COMICS CODE AUTHORITY
MATT GROENING
J.HO
SERBAN

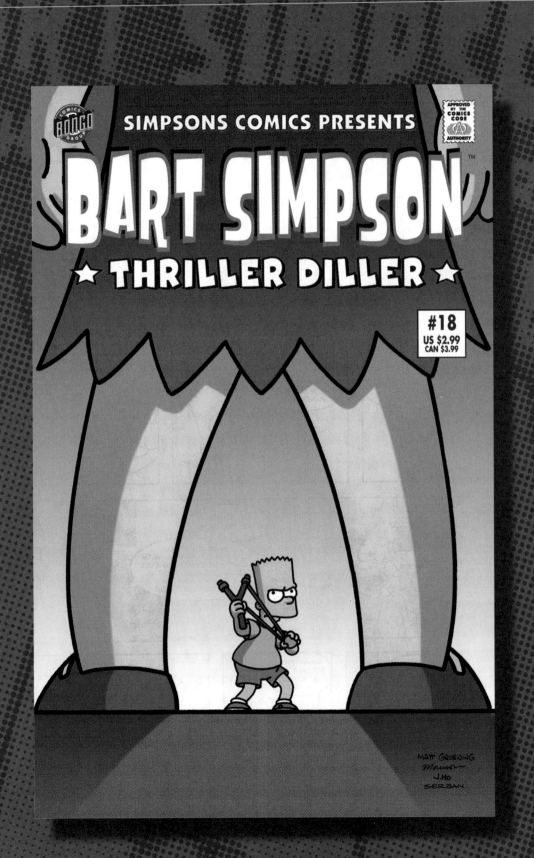

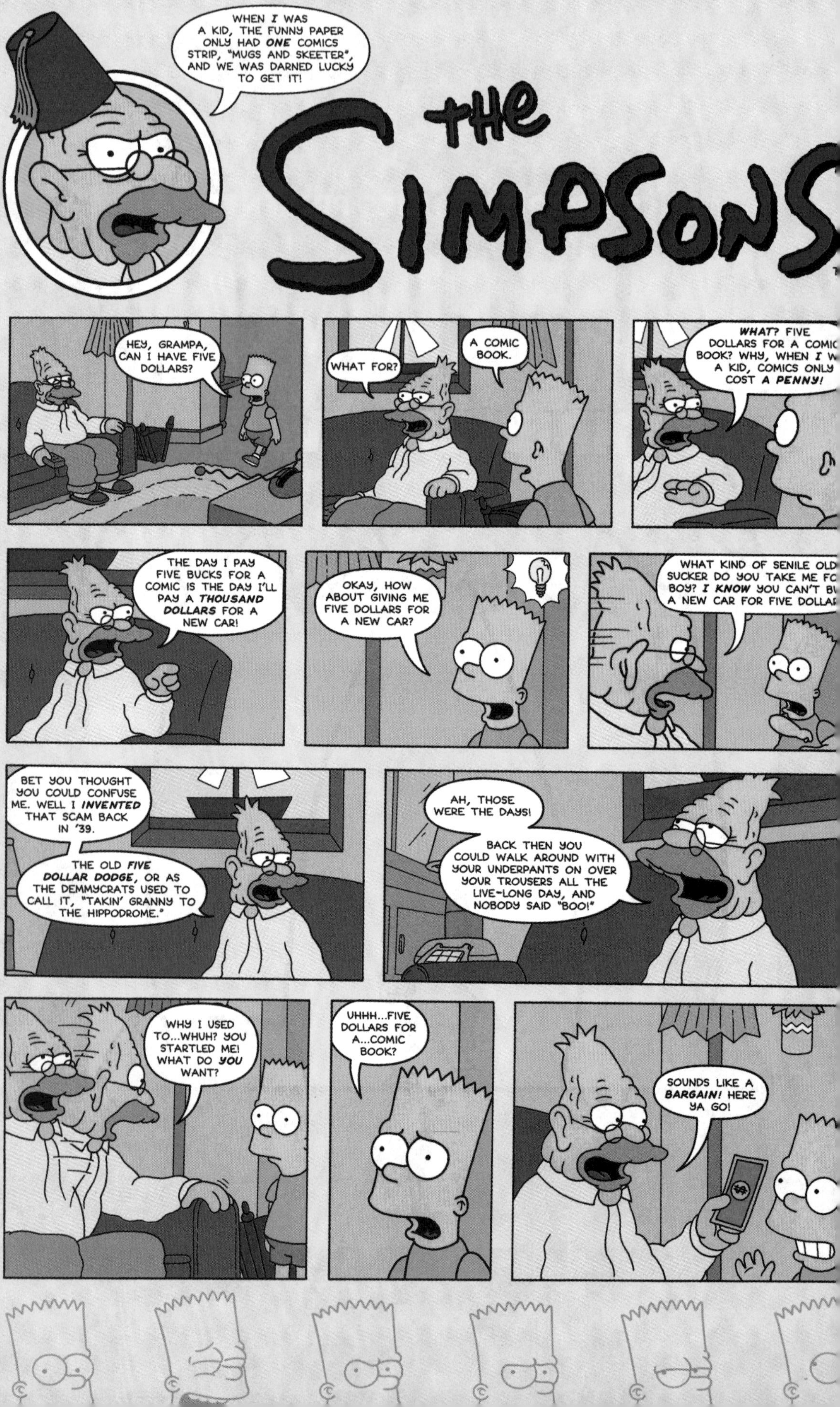

WHEN I WAS A KID, THE FUNNY PAPER ONLY HAD ONE COMICS STRIP, "MUGS AND SKEETER", AND WE WAS DARNED LUCKY TO GET IT!
THE SIMPSONS
HEY, GRAMPA, CAN I HAVE FIVE DOLLARS?
WHAT FOR?
A COMIC BOOK.
WHAT? FIVE DOLLARS FOR A COMIC BOOK? WHY, WHEN I W A KID, COMICS ONLY COST A PENNY!
THE DAY I PAY FIVE BUCKS FOR A COMIC IS THE DAY I'LL PAY A THOUSAND DOLLARS FOR A NEW CAR!
OKAY, HOW ABOUT GIVING ME FIVE DOLLARS FOR A NEW CAR?
WHAT KIND OF SENILE OLD SUCKER DO YOU TAKE ME FO BOY? I KNOW YOU CAN'T BU A NEW CAR FOR FIVE DOLLAR
BET YOU THOUGHT YOU COULD CONFUSE ME. WELL I INVENTED THAT SCAM BACK IN '39.
THE OLD FIVE DOLLAR DODGE, OR AS THE DEMMYCRATS USED TO CALL IT, "TAKIN' GRANNY TO THE HIPPODROME."
AH, THOSE WERE THE DAYS!
BACK THEN YOU COULD WALK AROUND WITH YOUR UNDERPANTS ON OVER YOUR TROUSERS ALL THE LIVE-LONG DAY, AND NOBODY SAID "BOO!"
WHY I USED TO...WHUH? YOU STARTLED ME! WHAT DO YOU WANT?
UHHH...FIVE DOLLARS FOR A...COMIC BOOK?
SOUNDS LIKE A BARGAIN! HERE YA GO!

MATT GROENING presents

BART SIMPSON SECRET AGENT, MAN

(PART ONE)

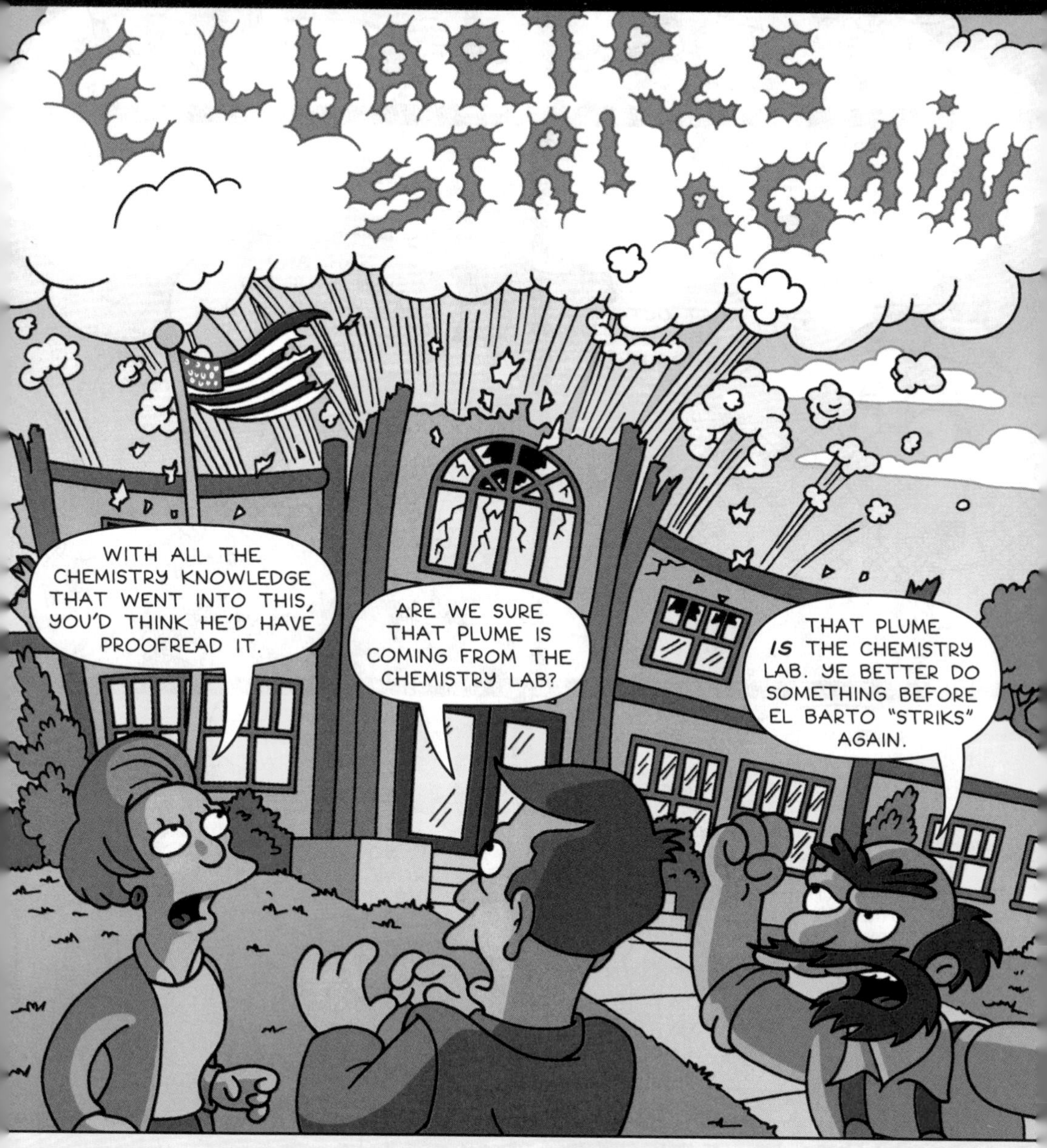

EL BARTO STRIKS AGAIN
WITH ALL THE CHEMISTRY KNOWLEDGE THAT WENT INTO THIS, YOU'D THINK HE'D HAVE PROOFREAD IT.
ARE WE SURE THAT PLUME IS COMING FROM THE CHEMISTRY LAB?
THAT PLUME *IS* THE CHEMISTRY LAB. YE BETTER DO SOMETHING BEFORE EL BARTO "STRIKS" AGAIN.

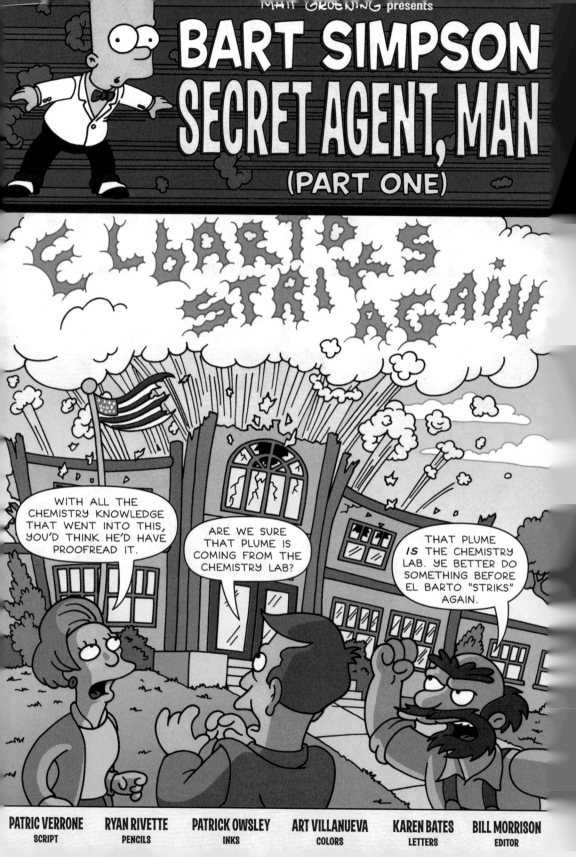

PATRIC VERRONE SCRIPT | **RYAN RIVETTE** PENCILS | **PATRICK OWSLEY** INKS | **ART VILLANUEVA** COLORS | **KAREN BATES** LETTERS | **BILL MORRISON** EDITOR

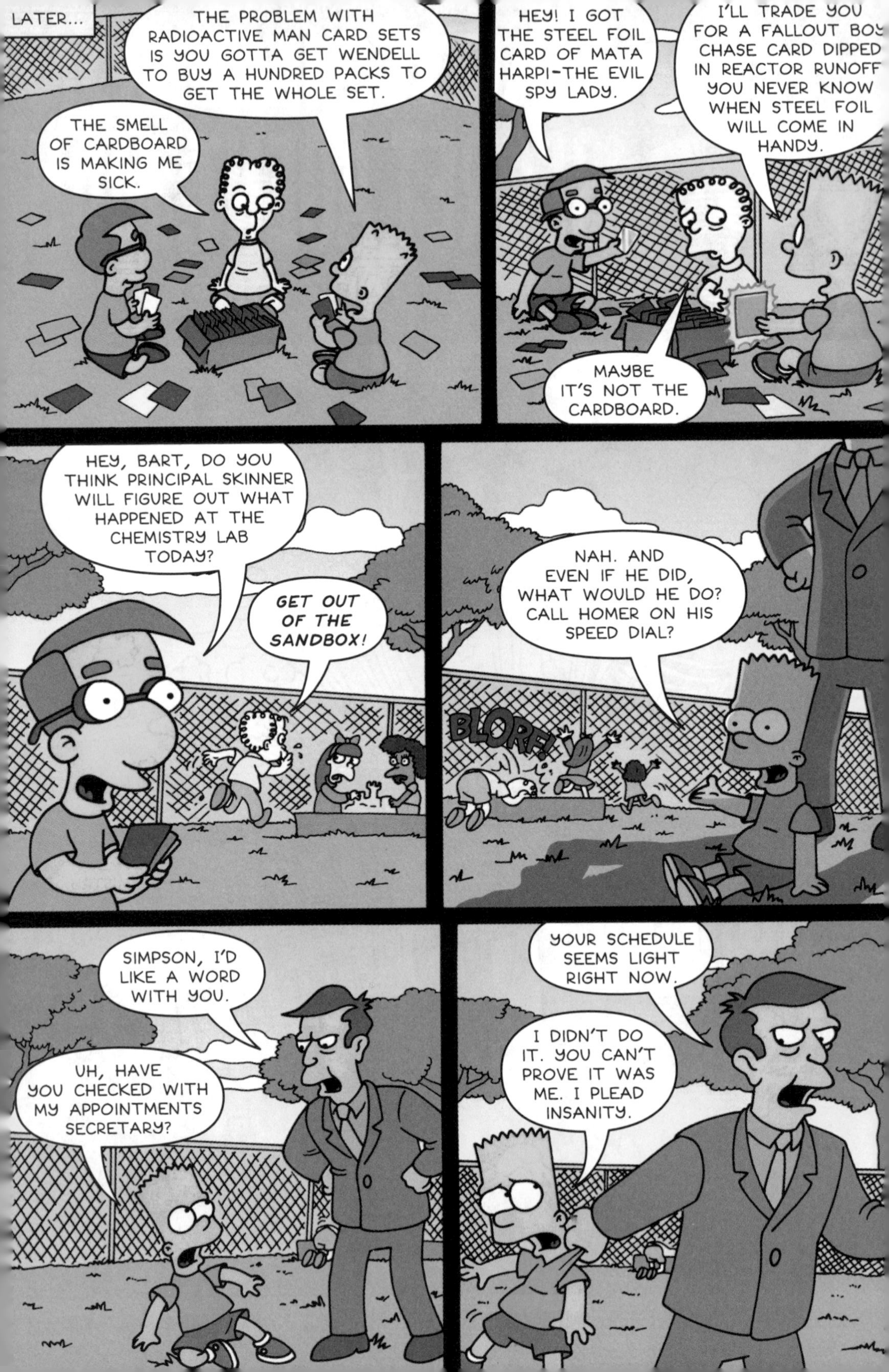
LATER...
THE PROBLEM WITH RADIOACTIVE MAN CARD SETS IS YOU GOTTA GET WENDELL TO BUY A HUNDRED PACKS TO GET THE WHOLE SET.
THE SMELL OF CARDBOARD IS MAKING ME SICK.
HEY! I GOT THE STEEL FOIL CARD OF MATA HARPI—THE EVIL SPY LADY.
I'LL TRADE YOU FOR A FALLOUT BOY CHASE CARD DIPPED IN REACTOR RUNOFF. YOU NEVER KNOW WHEN STEEL FOIL WILL COME IN HANDY.
MAYBE IT'S NOT THE CARDBOARD.
HEY, BART, DO YOU THINK PRINCIPAL SKINNER WILL FIGURE OUT WHAT HAPPENED AT THE CHEMISTRY LAB TODAY?
GET OUT OF THE SANDBOX!
NAH. AND EVEN IF HE DID, WHAT WOULD HE DO? CALL HOMER ON HIS SPEED DIAL?
BLORF!
SIMPSON, I'D LIKE A WORD WITH YOU.
UH, HAVE YOU CHECKED WITH MY APPOINTMENTS SECRETARY?
YOUR SCHEDULE SEEMS LIGHT RIGHT NOW.
I DIDN'T DO IT. YOU CAN'T PROVE IT WAS ME. I PLEAD INSANITY.

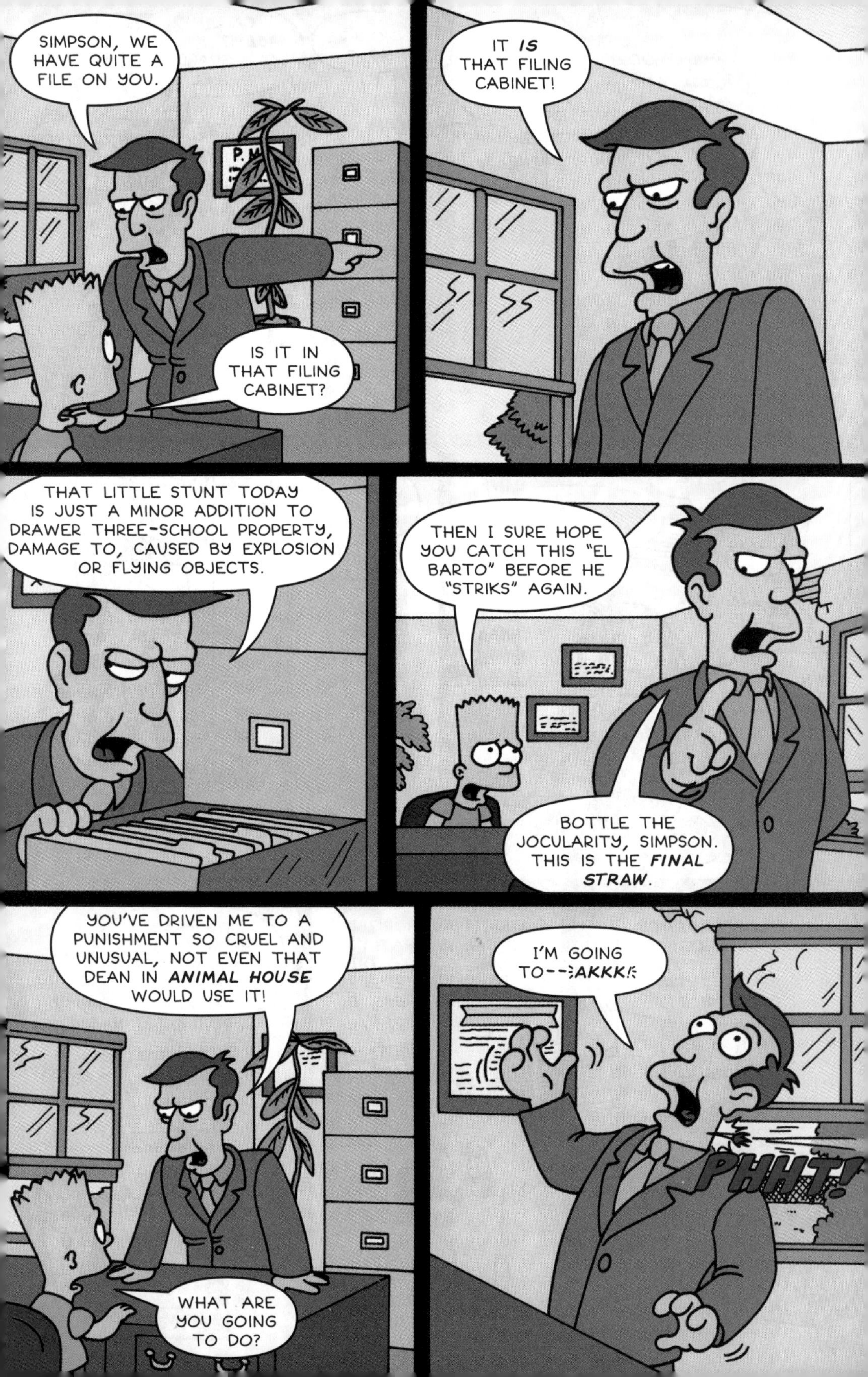
SIMPSON, WE HAVE QUITE A FILE ON YOU.
IS IT IN THAT FILING CABINET?
IT *IS* THAT FILING CABINET!
THAT LITTLE STUNT TODAY IS JUST A MINOR ADDITION TO DRAWER THREE-SCHOOL PROPERTY, DAMAGE TO, CAUSED BY EXPLOSION OR FLYING OBJECTS.
THEN I SURE HOPE YOU CATCH THIS "EL BARTO" BEFORE HE "STRIKS" AGAIN.
BOTTLE THE JOCULARITY, SIMPSON. THIS IS THE ***FINAL STRAW***.
YOU'VE DRIVEN ME TO A PUNISHMENT SO CRUEL AND UNUSUAL, NOT EVEN THAT DEAN IN ***ANIMAL HOUSE*** WOULD USE IT!
WHAT ARE YOU GOING TO DO?
I'M GOING TO--***AKKK!***
PHHT!

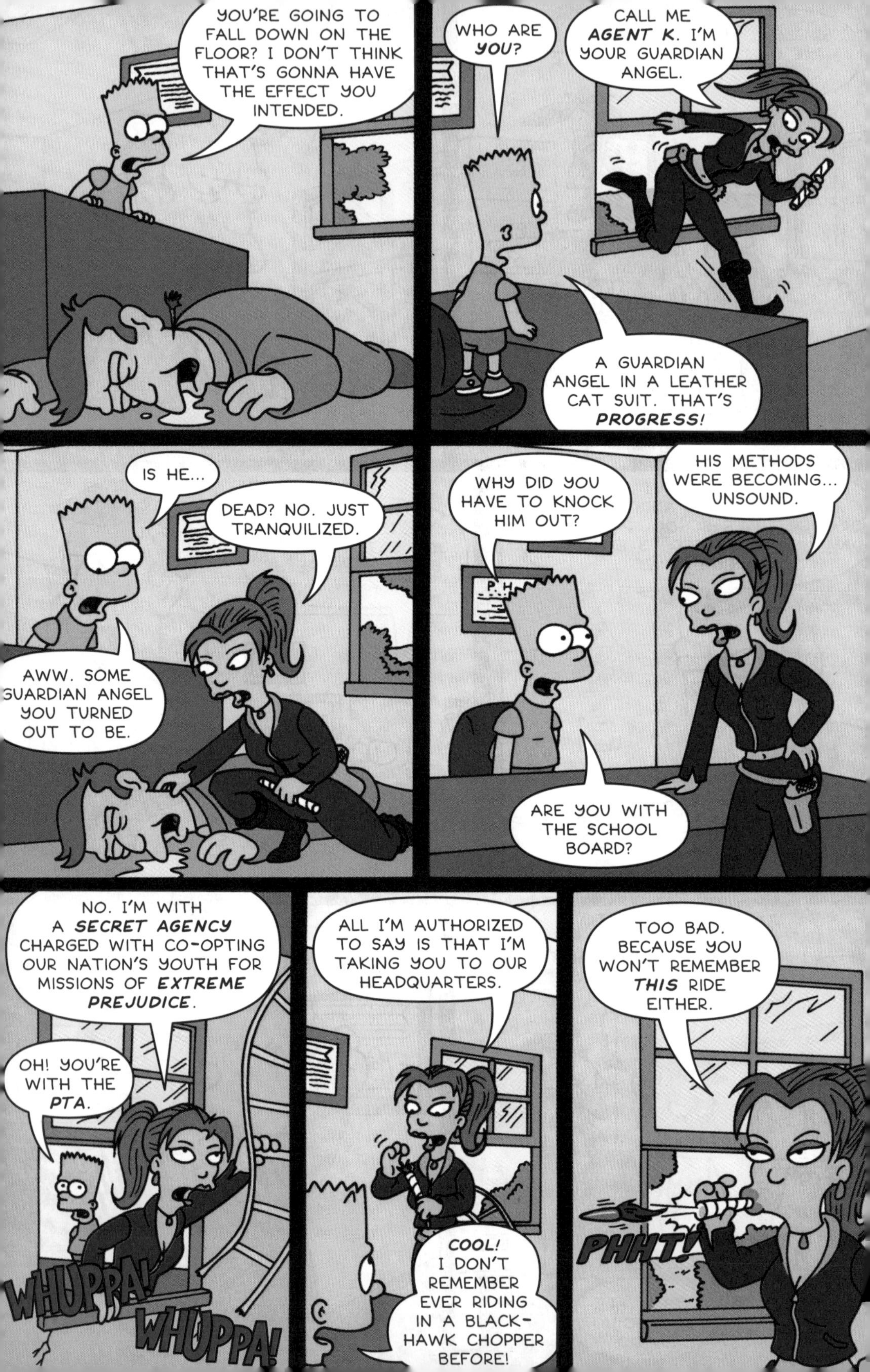

YOU'RE GOING TO FALL DOWN ON THE FLOOR? I DON'T THINK THAT'S GONNA HAVE THE EFFECT YOU INTENDED.
WHO ARE *YOU*?
CALL ME **AGENT K**. I'M YOUR GUARDIAN ANGEL.
A GUARDIAN ANGEL IN A LEATHER CAT SUIT. THAT'S ***PROGRESS!***
IS HE...
DEAD? NO. JUST TRANQUILIZED.
AWW. SOME GUARDIAN ANGEL YOU TURNED OUT TO BE.
WHY DID YOU HAVE TO KNOCK HIM OUT?
HIS METHODS WERE BECOMING... UNSOUND.
ARE YOU WITH THE SCHOOL BOARD?
NO. I'M WITH A ***SECRET AGENCY*** CHARGED WITH CO-OPTING OUR NATION'S YOUTH FOR MISSIONS OF ***EXTREME PREJUDICE***.
OH! YOU'RE WITH THE *PTA*.
WHUPPA! WHUPPA!
ALL I'M AUTHORIZED TO SAY IS THAT I'M TAKING YOU TO OUR HEADQUARTERS.
COOL! I DON'T REMEMBER EVER RIDING IN A BLACK-HAWK CHOPPER BEFORE!
TOO BAD. BECAUSE YOU WON'T REMEMBER ***THIS*** RIDE EITHER.
PHHT!

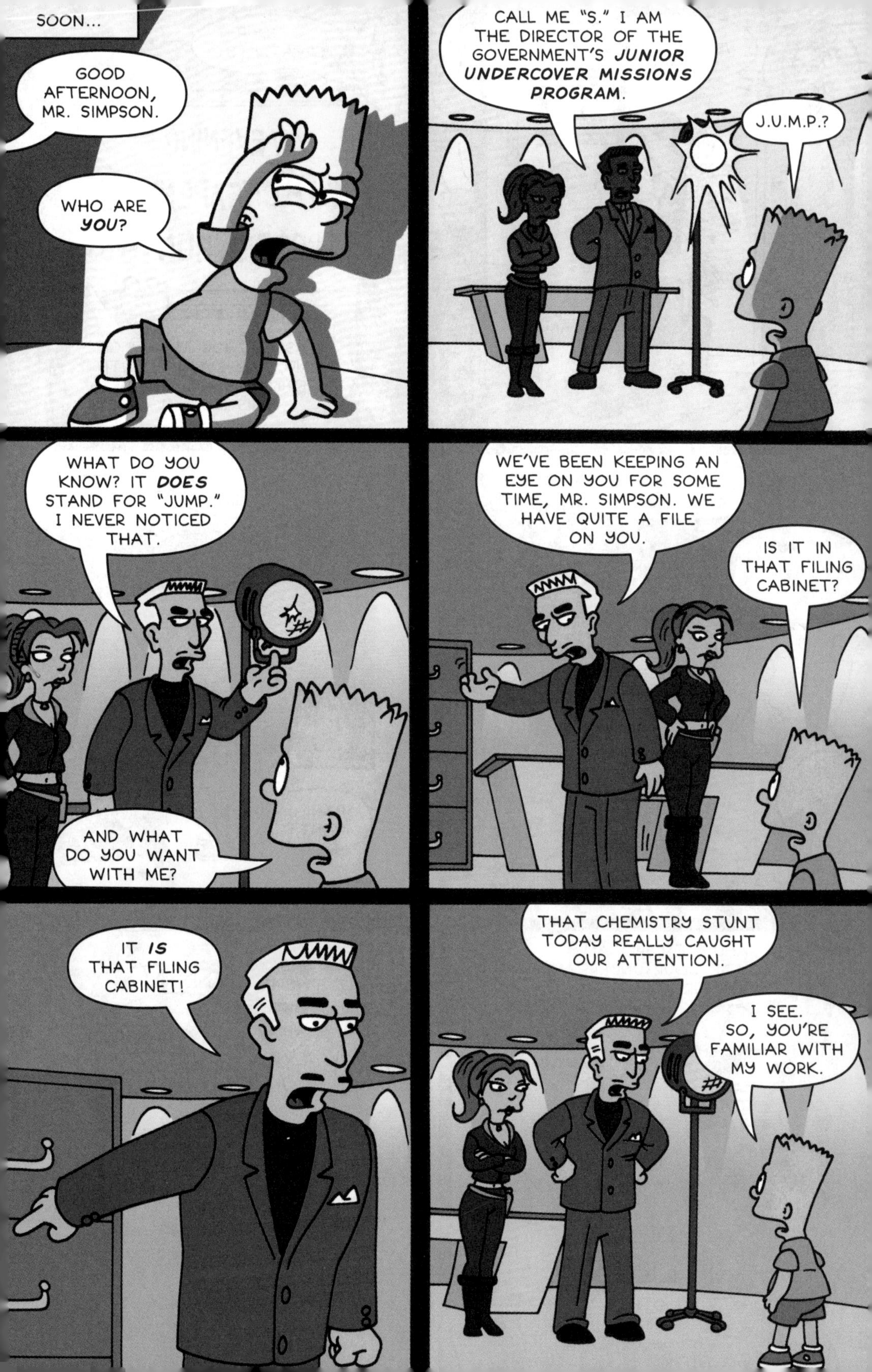
SOON...
GOOD AFTERNOON, MR. SIMPSON.
WHO ARE YOU?
CALL ME "S." I AM THE DIRECTOR OF THE GOVERNMENT'S JUNIOR UNDERCOVER MISSIONS PROGRAM.
J.U.M.P.?
WHAT DO YOU KNOW? IT DOES STAND FOR "JUMP." I NEVER NOTICED THAT.
AND WHAT DO YOU WANT WITH ME?
WE'VE BEEN KEEPING AN EYE ON YOU FOR SOME TIME, MR. SIMPSON. WE HAVE QUITE A FILE ON YOU.
IS IT IN THAT FILING CABINET?
IT IS THAT FILING CABINET!
THAT CHEMISTRY STUNT TODAY REALLY CAUGHT OUR ATTENTION.
I SEE. SO, YOU'RE FAMILIAR WITH MY WORK.

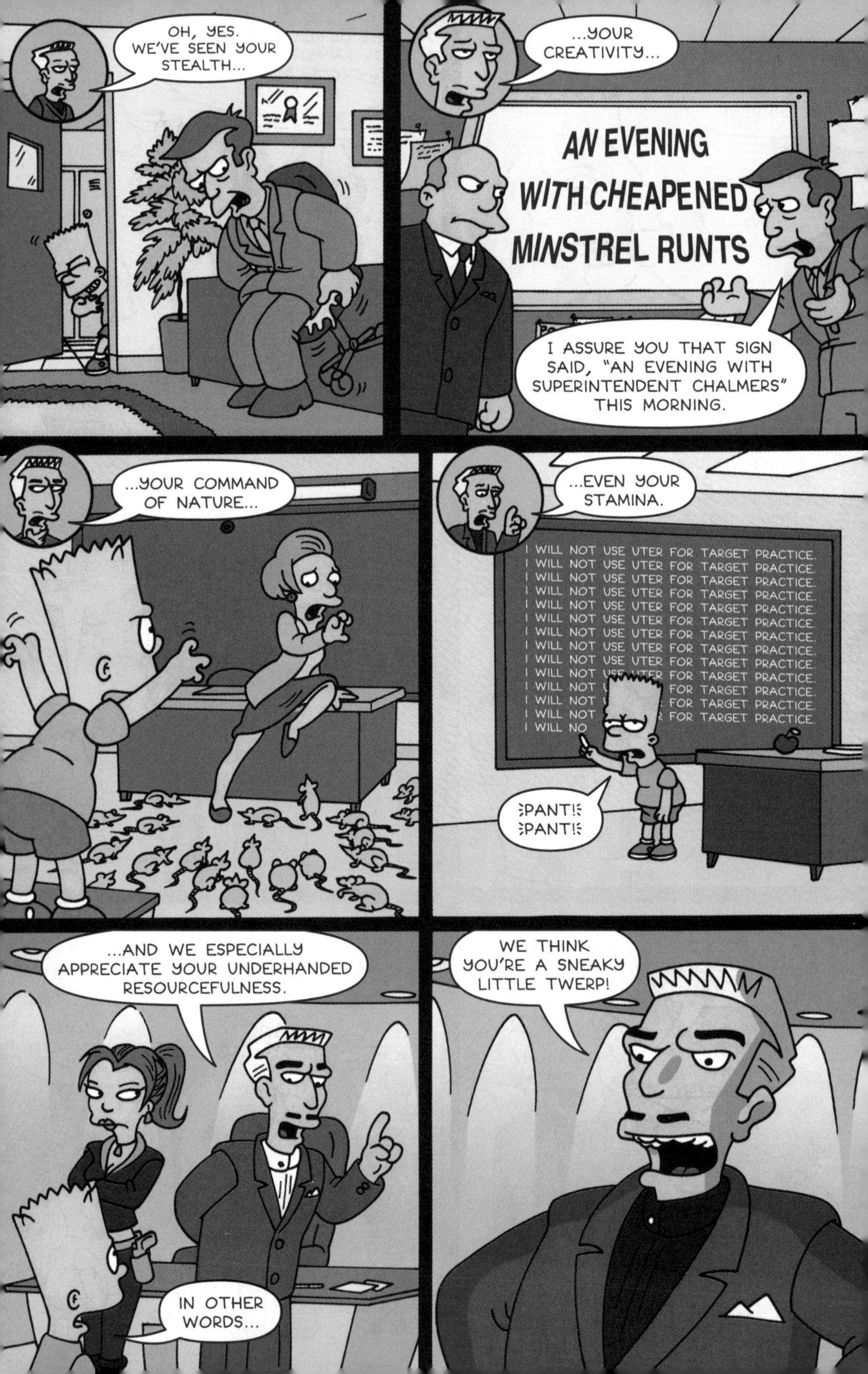

OH, YES. WE'VE SEEN YOUR STEALTH...
...YOUR CREATIVITY...
AN EVENING WITH CHEAPENED MINSTREL RUNTS
I ASSURE YOU THAT SIGN SAID, "AN EVENING WITH SUPERINTENDENT CHALMERS" THIS MORNING.
...YOUR COMMAND OF NATURE...
...EVEN YOUR STAMINA.
I WILL NOT USE UTER FOR TARGET PRACTICE.
I WILL NOT USE UTER FOR TARGET PRACTICE.
I WILL NOT USE UTER FOR TARGET PRACTICE.
I WILL NOT USE UTER FOR TARGET PRACTICE.
I WILL NOT USE UTER FOR TARGET PRACTICE.
I WILL NOT USE UTER FOR TARGET PRACTICE.
I WILL NOT USE UTER FOR TARGET PRACTICE.
I WILL NOT USE UTER FOR TARGET PRACTICE.
I WILL NOT USE UTER FOR TARGET PRACTICE.
I WILL NO
PANT! PANT!
...AND WE ESPECIALLY APPRECIATE YOUR UNDERHANDED RESOURCEFULNESS.
IN OTHER WORDS...
WE THINK YOU'RE A SNEAKY LITTLE TWERP!

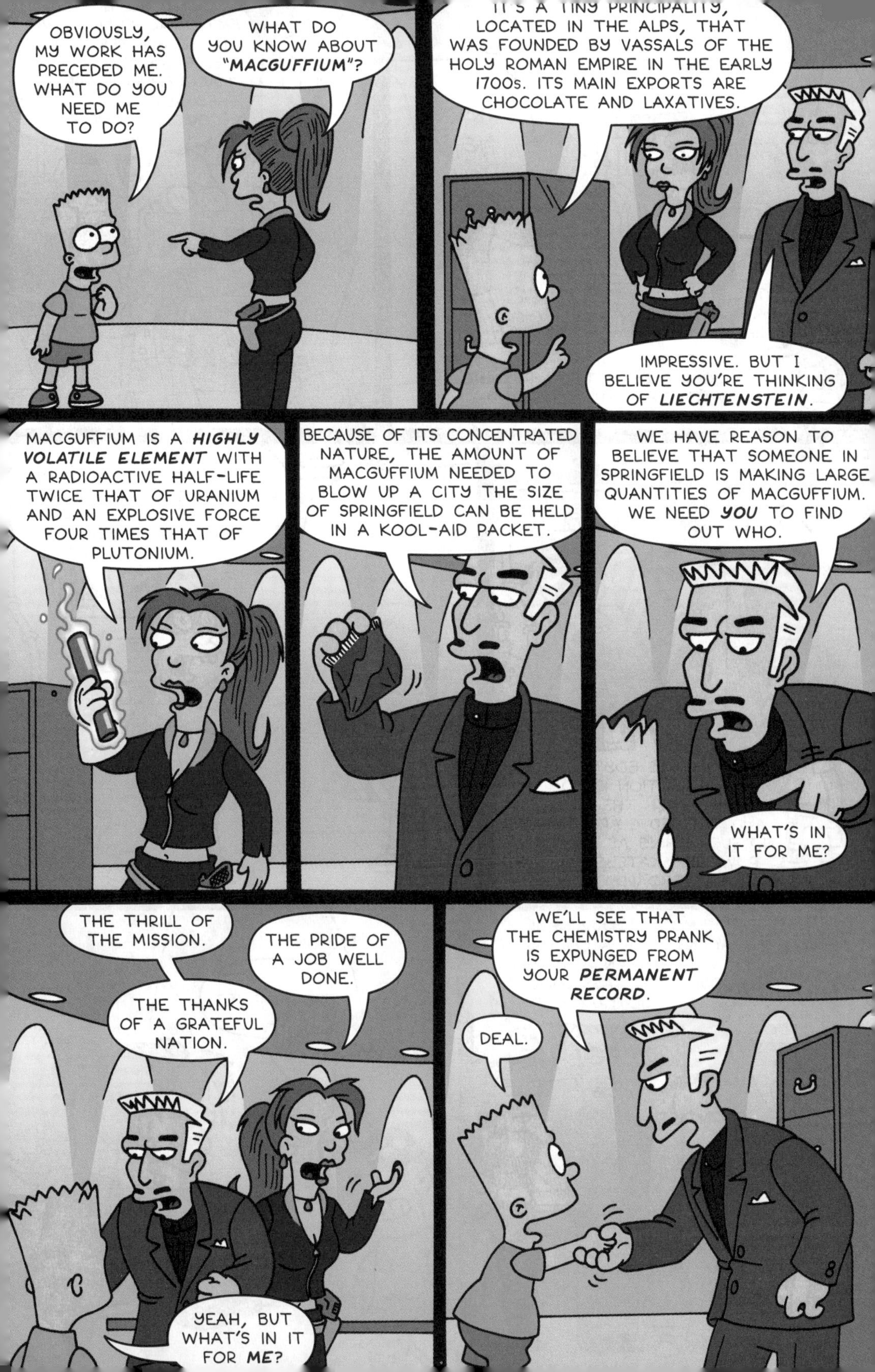
OBVIOUSLY, MY WORK HAS PRECEDED ME. WHAT DO YOU NEED ME TO DO?
WHAT DO YOU KNOW ABOUT "MACGUFFIUM"?
IT'S A TINY PRINCIPALITY, LOCATED IN THE ALPS, THAT WAS FOUNDED BY VASSALS OF THE HOLY ROMAN EMPIRE IN THE EARLY 1700s. ITS MAIN EXPORTS ARE CHOCOLATE AND LAXATIVES.
IMPRESSIVE. BUT I BELIEVE YOU'RE THINKING OF LIECHTENSTEIN.
MACGUFFIUM IS A HIGHLY VOLATILE ELEMENT WITH A RADIOACTIVE HALF-LIFE TWICE THAT OF URANIUM AND AN EXPLOSIVE FORCE FOUR TIMES THAT OF PLUTONIUM.
BECAUSE OF ITS CONCENTRATED NATURE, THE AMOUNT OF MACGUFFIUM NEEDED TO BLOW UP A CITY THE SIZE OF SPRINGFIELD CAN BE HELD IN A KOOL-AID PACKET.
WE HAVE REASON TO BELIEVE THAT SOMEONE IN SPRINGFIELD IS MAKING LARGE QUANTITIES OF MACGUFFIUM. WE NEED YOU TO FIND OUT WHO.
WHAT'S IN IT FOR ME?
THE THRILL OF THE MISSION.
THE PRIDE OF A JOB WELL DONE.
THE THANKS OF A GRATEFUL NATION.
YEAH, BUT WHAT'S IN IT FOR ME?
WE'LL SEE THAT THE CHEMISTRY PRANK IS EXPUNGED FROM YOUR PERMANENT RECORD.
DEAL.

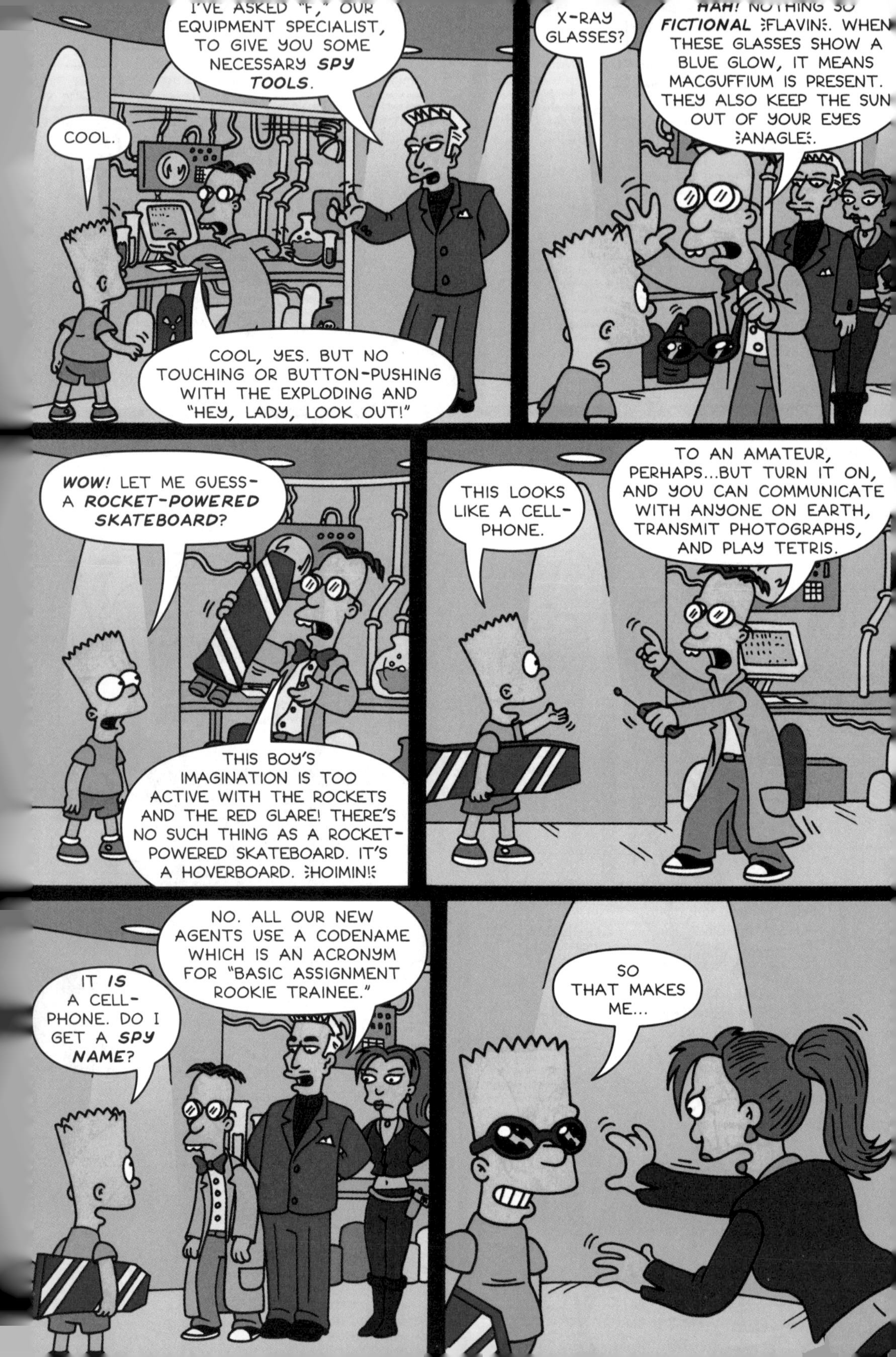
I'VE ASKED "F," OUR EQUIPMENT SPECIALIST, TO GIVE YOU SOME NECESSARY ***SPY TOOLS***.
COOL.
COOL, YES. BUT NO TOUCHING OR BUTTON-PUSHING WITH THE EXPLODING AND "HEY, LADY, LOOK OUT!"
X-RAY GLASSES?
HAH! NOTHING SO ***FICTIONAL*** ⁝FLAVIN⁝. WHEN THESE GLASSES SHOW A BLUE GLOW, IT MEANS MACGUFFIUM IS PRESENT. THEY ALSO KEEP THE SUN OUT OF YOUR EYES ⁝ANAGLE⁝.
WOW! LET ME GUESS- A ***ROCKET-POWERED SKATEBOARD***?
THIS BOY'S IMAGINATION IS TOO ACTIVE WITH THE ROCKETS AND THE RED GLARE! THERE'S NO SUCH THING AS A ROCKET-POWERED SKATEBOARD. IT'S A HOVERBOARD. ⁝HOIMIN!⁝
THIS LOOKS LIKE A CELL-PHONE.
TO AN AMATEUR, PERHAPS...BUT TURN IT ON, AND YOU CAN COMMUNICATE WITH ANYONE ON EARTH, TRANSMIT PHOTOGRAPHS, AND PLAY TETRIS.
IT ***IS*** A CELL-PHONE. DO I GET A ***SPY NAME***?
NO. ALL OUR NEW AGENTS USE A CODENAME WHICH IS AN ACRONYM FOR "BASIC ASSIGNMENT ROOKIE TRAINEE."
SO THAT MAKES ME...

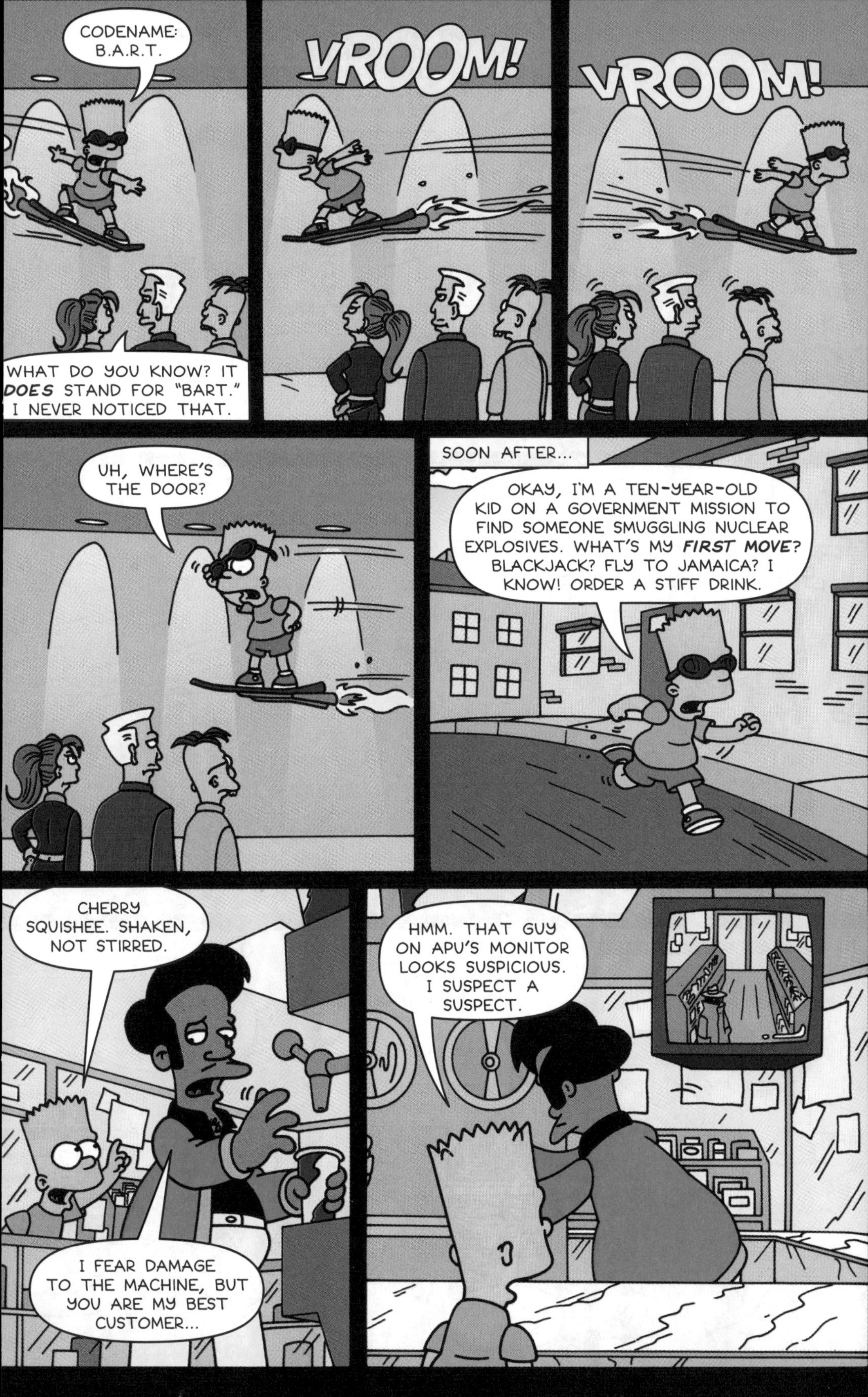
CODENAME: B.A.R.T.
WHAT DO YOU KNOW? IT DOES STAND FOR "BART." I NEVER NOTICED THAT.
VROOM!
VROOM!
UH, WHERE'S THE DOOR?
SOON AFTER...
OKAY, I'M A TEN-YEAR-OLD KID ON A GOVERNMENT MISSION TO FIND SOMEONE SMUGGLING NUCLEAR EXPLOSIVES. WHAT'S MY FIRST MOVE? BLACKJACK? FLY TO JAMAICA? I KNOW! ORDER A STIFF DRINK.
CHERRY SQUISHEE. SHAKEN, NOT STIRRED.
I FEAR DAMAGE TO THE MACHINE, BUT YOU ARE MY BEST CUSTOMER...
HMM. THAT GUY ON APU'S MONITOR LOOKS SUSPICIOUS. I SUSPECT A SUSPECT.

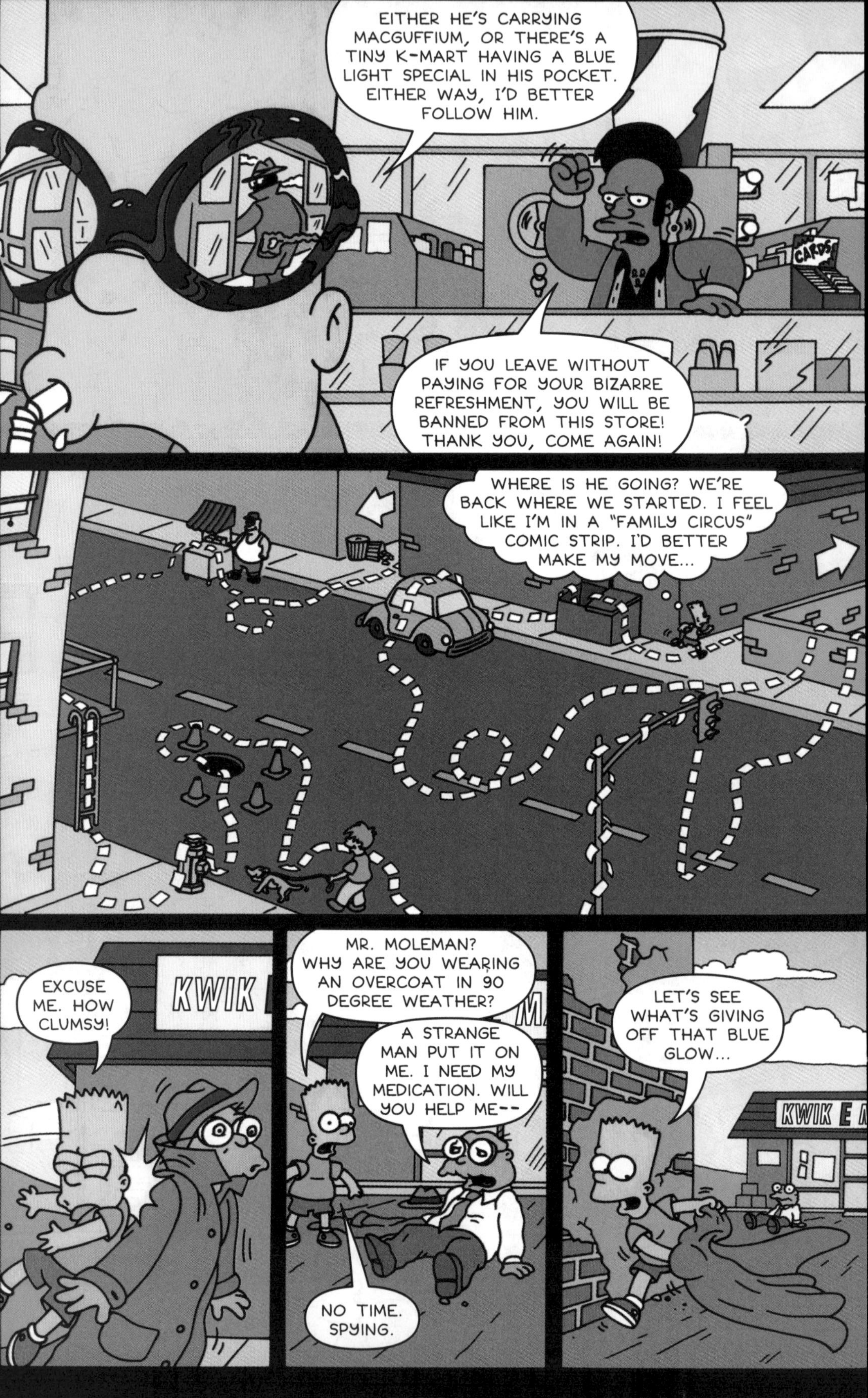
EITHER HE'S CARRYING MACGUFFIUM, OR THERE'S A TINY K-MART HAVING A BLUE LIGHT SPECIAL IN HIS POCKET. EITHER WAY, I'D BETTER FOLLOW HIM.
CARDS
IF YOU LEAVE WITHOUT PAYING FOR YOUR BIZARRE REFRESHMENT, YOU WILL BE BANNED FROM THIS STORE! THANK YOU, COME AGAIN!
WHERE IS HE GOING? WE'RE BACK WHERE WE STARTED. I FEEL LIKE I'M IN A "FAMILY CIRCUS" COMIC STRIP. I'D BETTER MAKE MY MOVE...
KWIK
EXCUSE ME. HOW CLUMSY!
MR. MOLEMAN? WHY ARE YOU WEARING AN OVERCOAT IN 90 DEGREE WEATHER?
A STRANGE MAN PUT IT ON ME. I NEED MY MEDICATION. WILL YOU HELP ME--
NO TIME. SPYING.
LET'S SEE WHAT'S GIVING OFF THAT BLUE GLOW...
KWIK E

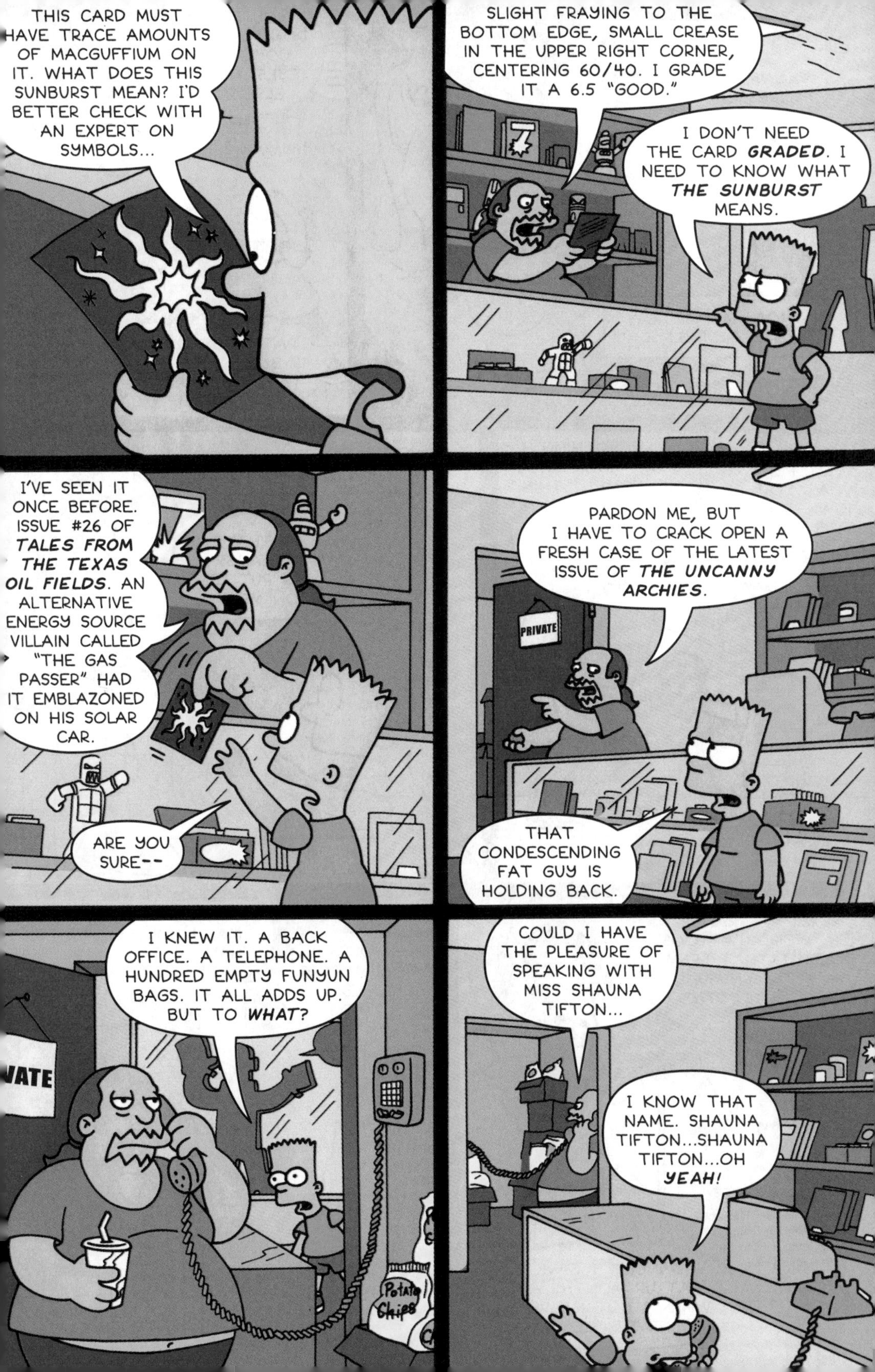
THIS CARD MUST HAVE TRACE AMOUNTS OF MACGUFFIUM ON IT. WHAT DOES THIS SUNBURST MEAN? I'D BETTER CHECK WITH AN EXPERT ON SYMBOLS...
SLIGHT FRAYING TO THE BOTTOM EDGE, SMALL CREASE IN THE UPPER RIGHT CORNER, CENTERING 60/40. I GRADE IT A 6.5 "GOOD."
I DON'T NEED THE CARD ***GRADED***. I NEED TO KNOW WHAT ***THE SUNBURST*** MEANS.
I'VE SEEN IT ONCE BEFORE. ISSUE #26 OF ***TALES FROM THE TEXAS OIL FIELDS***. AN ALTERNATIVE ENERGY SOURCE VILLAIN CALLED "THE GAS PASSER" HAD IT EMBLAZONED ON HIS SOLAR CAR.
ARE YOU SURE--
PARDON ME, BUT I HAVE TO CRACK OPEN A FRESH CASE OF THE LATEST ISSUE OF ***THE UNCANNY ARCHIES***.
PRIVATE
THAT CONDESCENDING FAT GUY IS HOLDING BACK.
I KNEW IT. A BACK OFFICE. A TELEPHONE. A HUNDRED EMPTY FUNYUN BAGS. IT ALL ADDS UP. BUT TO ***WHAT***?
VATE
Potato Chips
COULD I HAVE THE PLEASURE OF SPEAKING WITH MISS SHAUNA TIFTON...
I KNOW THAT NAME. SHAUNA TIFTON...SHAUNA TIFTON...OH ***YEAH***!

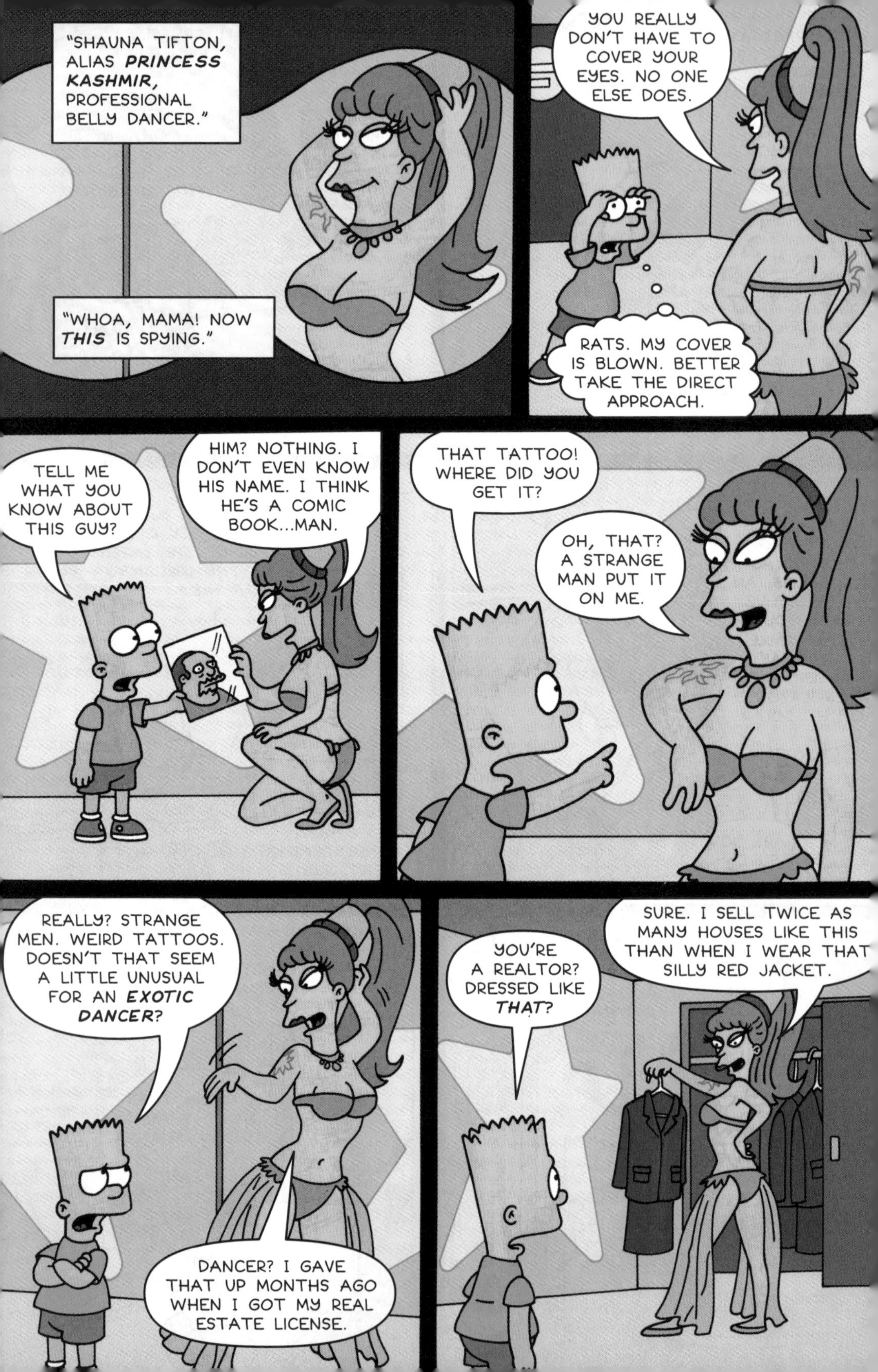
"SHAUNA TIFTON, ALIAS PRINCESS KASHMIR, PROFESSIONAL BELLY DANCER."
"WHOA, MAMA! NOW THIS IS SPYING."
YOU REALLY DON'T HAVE TO COVER YOUR EYES. NO ONE ELSE DOES.
RATS. MY COVER IS BLOWN. BETTER TAKE THE DIRECT APPROACH.
TELL ME WHAT YOU KNOW ABOUT THIS GUY?
HIM? NOTHING. I DON'T EVEN KNOW HIS NAME. I THINK HE'S A COMIC BOOK...MAN.
THAT TATTOO! WHERE DID YOU GET IT?
OH, THAT? A STRANGE MAN PUT IT ON ME.
REALLY? STRANGE MEN. WEIRD TATTOOS. DOESN'T THAT SEEM A LITTLE UNUSUAL FOR AN EXOTIC DANCER?
DANCER? I GAVE THAT UP MONTHS AGO WHEN I GOT MY REAL ESTATE LICENSE.
YOU'RE A REALTOR? DRESSED LIKE THAT?
SURE. I SELL TWICE AS MANY HOUSES LIKE THIS THAN WHEN I WEAR THAT SILLY RED JACKET.

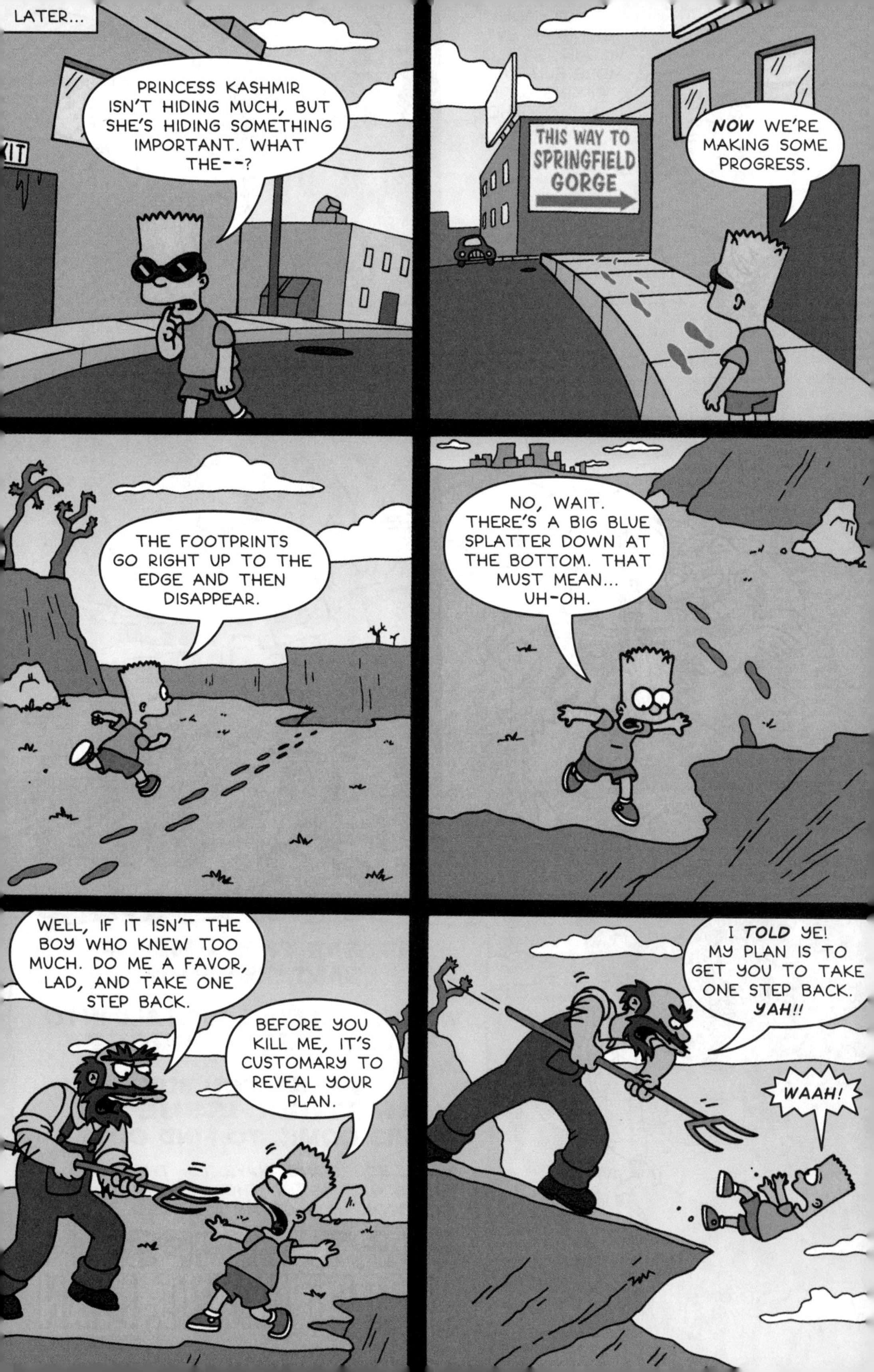
LATER...
PRINCESS KASHMIR ISN'T HIDING MUCH, BUT SHE'S HIDING SOMETHING IMPORTANT. WHAT THE--?
THIS WAY TO SPRINGFIELD GORGE
NOW WE'RE MAKING SOME PROGRESS.
THE FOOTPRINTS GO RIGHT UP TO THE EDGE AND THEN DISAPPEAR.
NO, WAIT. THERE'S A BIG BLUE SPLATTER DOWN AT THE BOTTOM. THAT MUST MEAN... UH-OH.
WELL, IF IT ISN'T THE BOY WHO KNEW TOO MUCH. DO ME A FAVOR, LAD, AND TAKE ONE STEP BACK.
BEFORE YOU KILL ME, IT'S CUSTOMARY TO REVEAL YOUR PLAN.
I TOLD YE! MY PLAN IS TO GET YOU TO TAKE ONE STEP BACK. YAH!!
WAAH!

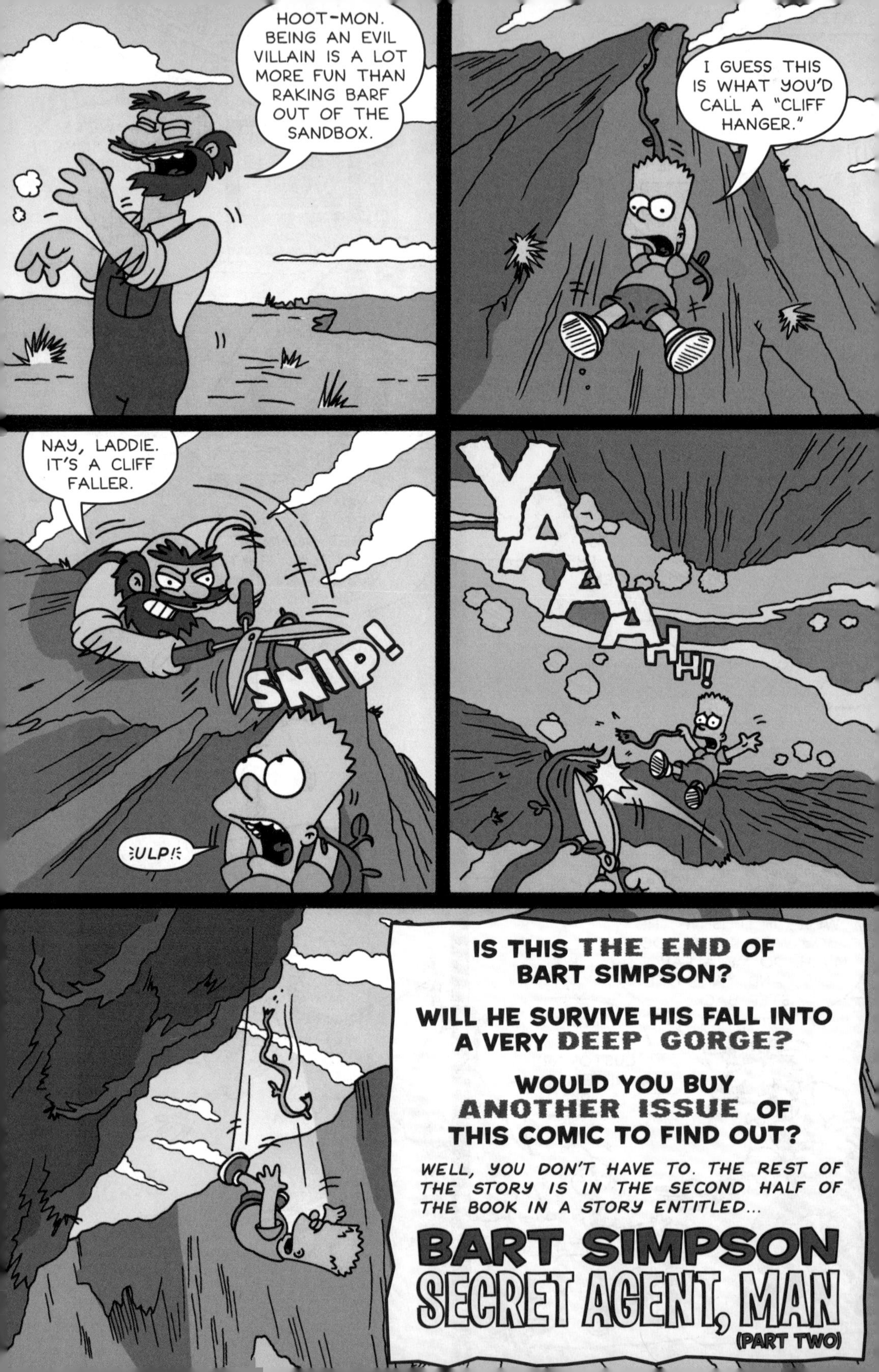

HOOT-MON. BEING AN EVIL VILLAIN IS A LOT MORE FUN THAN RAKING BARF OUT OF THE SANDBOX.
I GUESS THIS IS WHAT YOU'D CALL A "CLIFF HANGER."
NAY, LADDIE. IT'S A CLIFF FALLER.
SNIP!
ULP!
YAAAHH!
IS THIS THE END OF BART SIMPSON?
WILL HE SURVIVE HIS FALL INTO A VERY DEEP GORGE?
WOULD YOU BUY ANOTHER ISSUE OF THIS COMIC TO FIND OUT?
WELL, YOU DON'T HAVE TO. THE REST OF THE STORY IS IN THE SECOND HALF OF THE BOOK IN A STORY ENTITLED...
BART SIMPSON
SECRET AGENT, MAN
(PART TWO)

ITCHY & SCRATCHY in THE TRUTH ABOUT CATS AND MICE

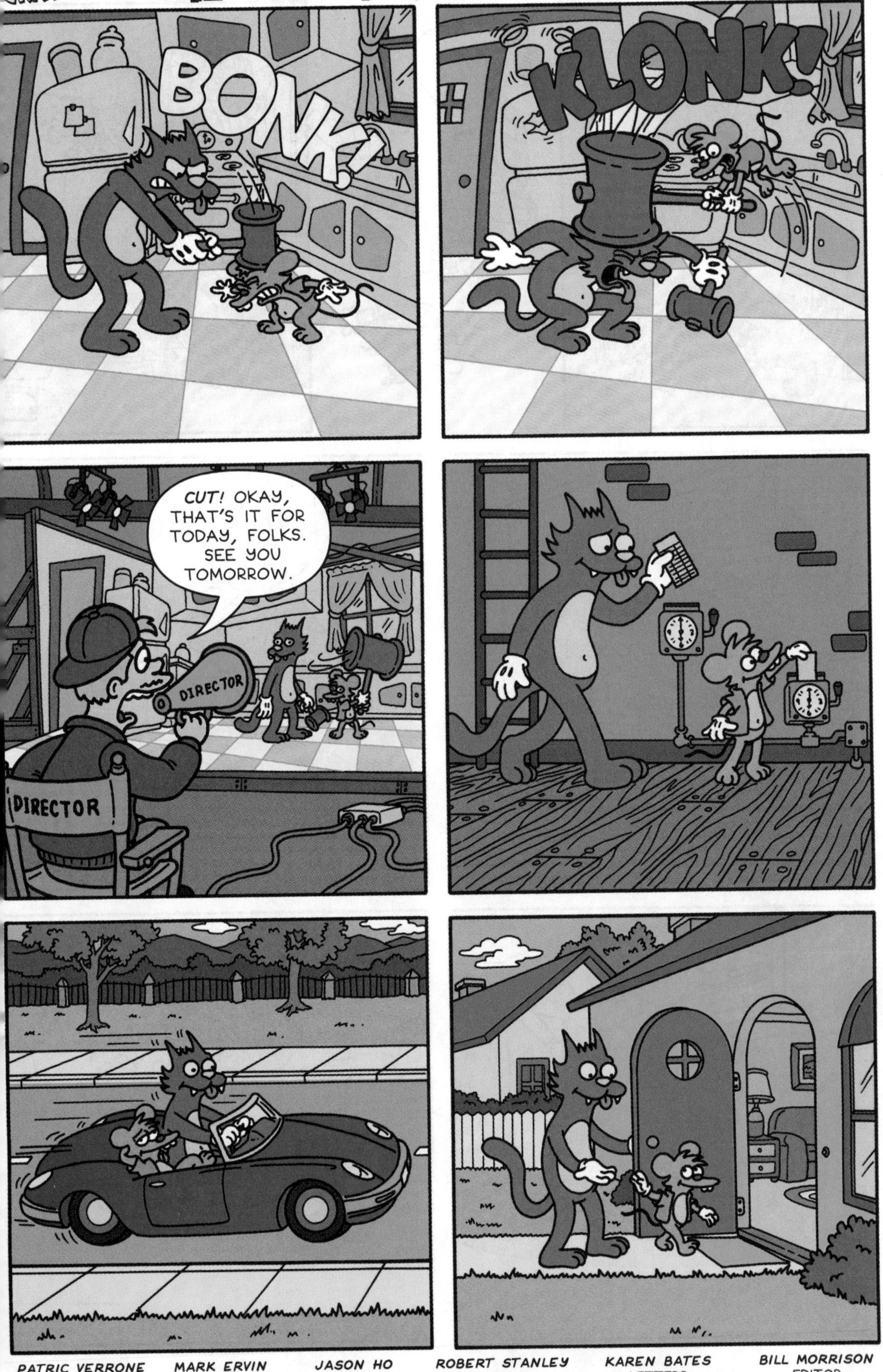
BONK!
KLONK!
CUT! OKAY, THAT'S IT FOR TODAY, FOLKS. SEE YOU TOMORROW.
DIRECTOR
DIRECTOR

PATRIC VERRONE SCRIPT | MARK ERVIN PENCILS | JASON HO INKS | ROBERT STANLEY COLORS | KAREN BATES LETTERS | BILL MORRISON EDITOR

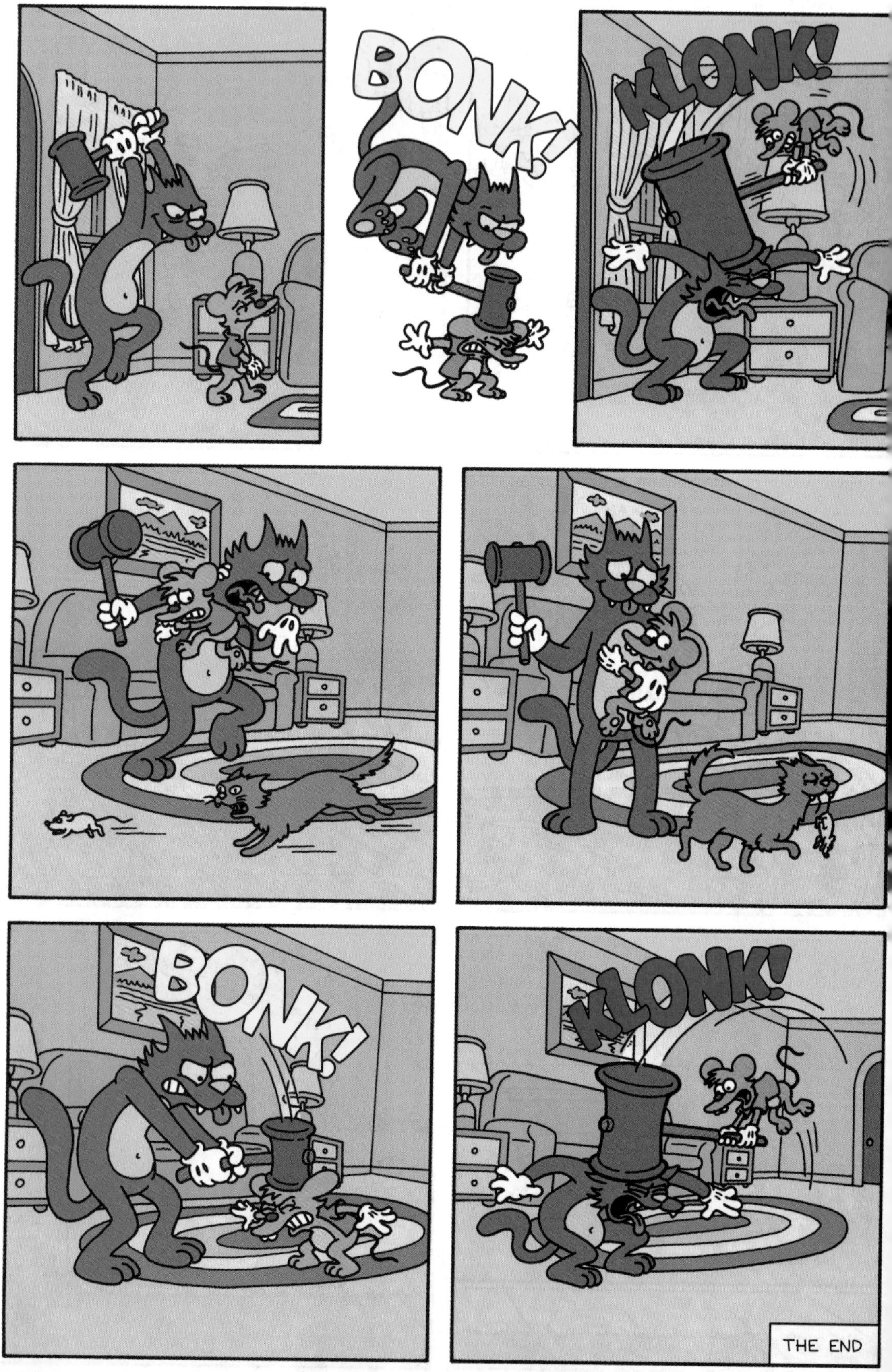
BONK!
KLONK!
BONK!
KLONK!
THE END

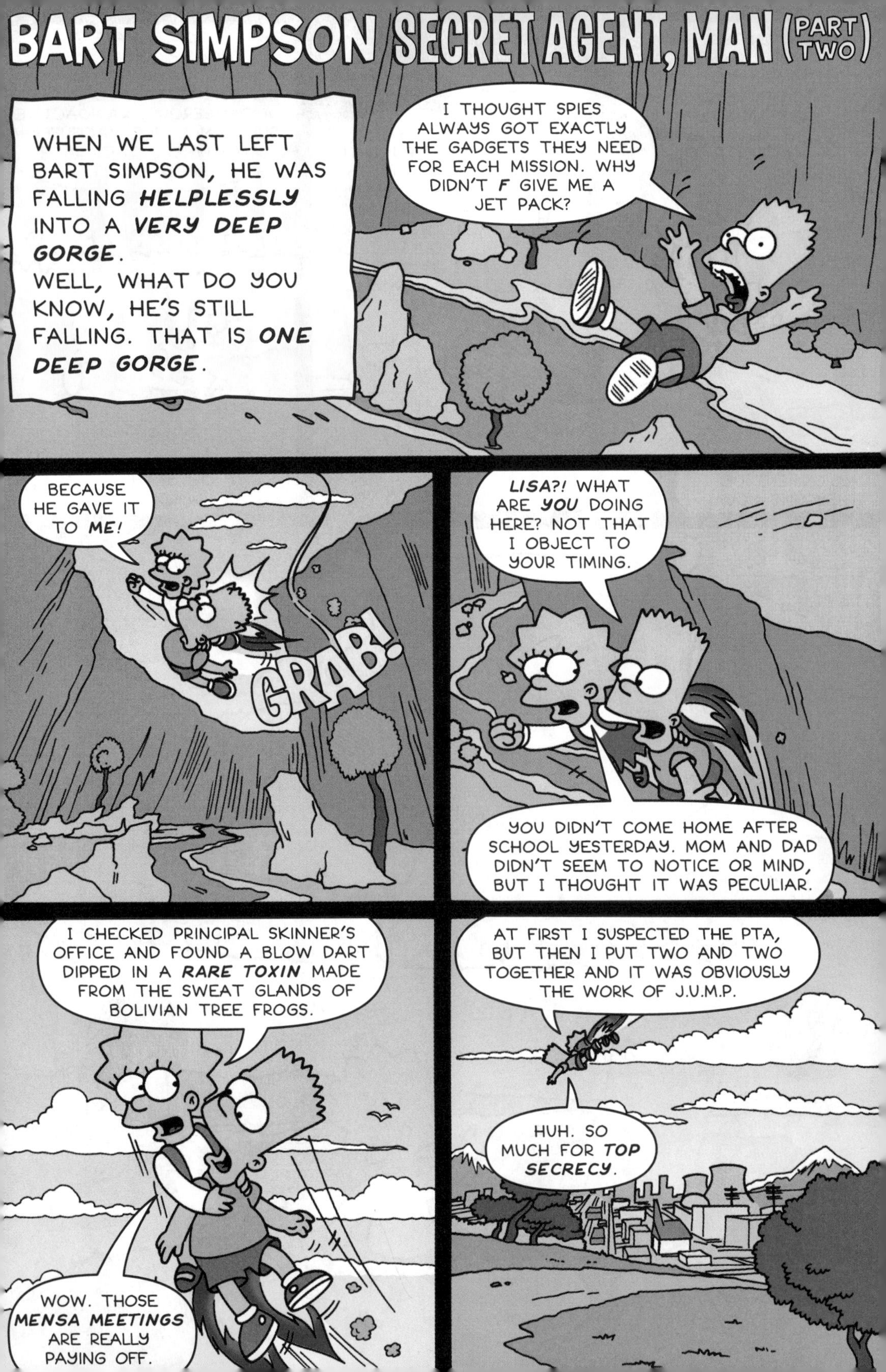
BART SIMPSON SECRET AGENT, MAN (PART TWO)
WHEN WE LAST LEFT BART SIMPSON, HE WAS FALLING HELPLESSLY INTO A VERY DEEP GORGE. WELL, WHAT DO YOU KNOW, HE'S STILL FALLING. THAT IS ONE DEEP GORGE.
I THOUGHT SPIES ALWAYS GOT EXACTLY THE GADGETS THEY NEED FOR EACH MISSION. WHY DIDN'T F GIVE ME A JET PACK?
BECAUSE HE GAVE IT TO ME!
GRAB!
LISA?! WHAT ARE YOU DOING HERE? NOT THAT I OBJECT TO YOUR TIMING.
YOU DIDN'T COME HOME AFTER SCHOOL YESTERDAY. MOM AND DAD DIDN'T SEEM TO NOTICE OR MIND, BUT I THOUGHT IT WAS PECULIAR.
I CHECKED PRINCIPAL SKINNER'S OFFICE AND FOUND A BLOW DART DIPPED IN A RARE TOXIN MADE FROM THE SWEAT GLANDS OF BOLIVIAN TREE FROGS.
WOW. THOSE MENSA MEETINGS ARE REALLY PAYING OFF.
AT FIRST I SUSPECTED THE PTA, BUT THEN I PUT TWO AND TWO TOGETHER AND IT WAS OBVIOUSLY THE WORK OF J.U.M.P.
HUH. SO MUCH FOR TOP SECRECY.

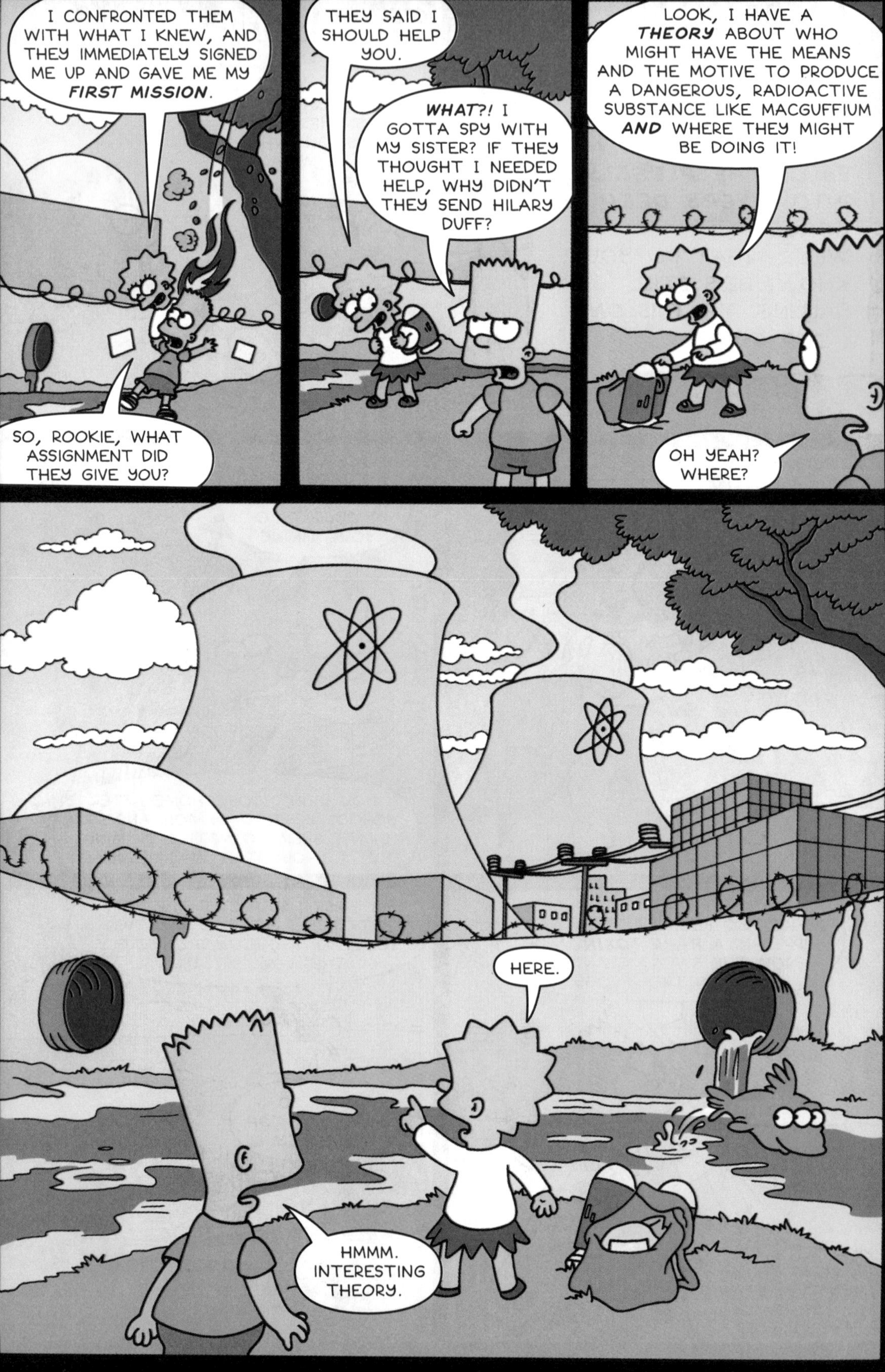
I CONFRONTED THEM WITH WHAT I KNEW, AND THEY IMMEDIATELY SIGNED ME UP AND GAVE ME MY FIRST MISSION.
SO, ROOKIE, WHAT ASSIGNMENT DID THEY GIVE YOU?
THEY SAID I SHOULD HELP YOU.
WHAT?! I GOTTA SPY WITH MY SISTER? IF THEY THOUGHT I NEEDED HELP, WHY DIDN'T THEY SEND HILARY DUFF?
LOOK, I HAVE A THEORY ABOUT WHO MIGHT HAVE THE MEANS AND THE MOTIVE TO PRODUCE A DANGEROUS, RADIOACTIVE SUBSTANCE LIKE MACGUFFIUM AND WHERE THEY MIGHT BE DOING IT!
OH YEAH? WHERE?
HERE.
HMMM. INTERESTING THEORY.

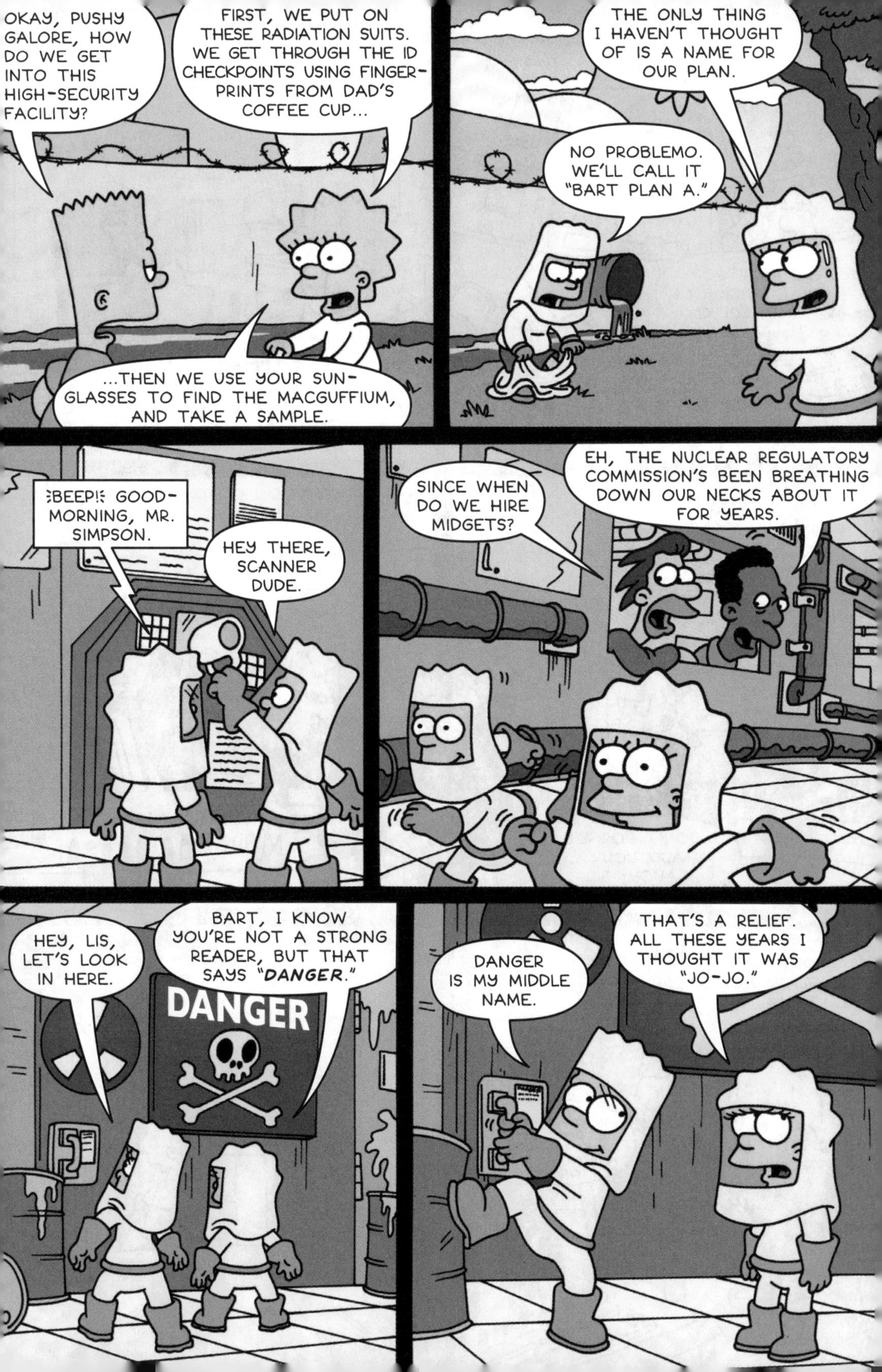
OKAY, PUSHY GALORE, HOW DO WE GET INTO THIS HIGH-SECURITY FACILITY?
FIRST, WE PUT ON THESE RADIATION SUITS. WE GET THROUGH THE ID CHECKPOINTS USING FINGER-PRINTS FROM DAD'S COFFEE CUP...
...THEN WE USE YOUR SUN-GLASSES TO FIND THE MACGUFFIUM, AND TAKE A SAMPLE.
THE ONLY THING I HAVEN'T THOUGHT OF IS A NAME FOR OUR PLAN.
NO PROBLEMO. WE'LL CALL IT "BART PLAN A."
BEEP! GOOD-MORNING, MR. SIMPSON.
HEY THERE, SCANNER DUDE.
SINCE WHEN DO WE HIRE MIDGETS?
EH, THE NUCLEAR REGULATORY COMMISSION'S BEEN BREATHING DOWN OUR NECKS ABOUT IT FOR YEARS.
HEY, LIS, LET'S LOOK IN HERE.
BART, I KNOW YOU'RE NOT A STRONG READER, BUT THAT SAYS "*DANGER*."
DANGER
DANGER IS MY MIDDLE NAME.
THAT'S A RELIEF. ALL THESE YEARS I THOUGHT IT WAS "JO-JO."

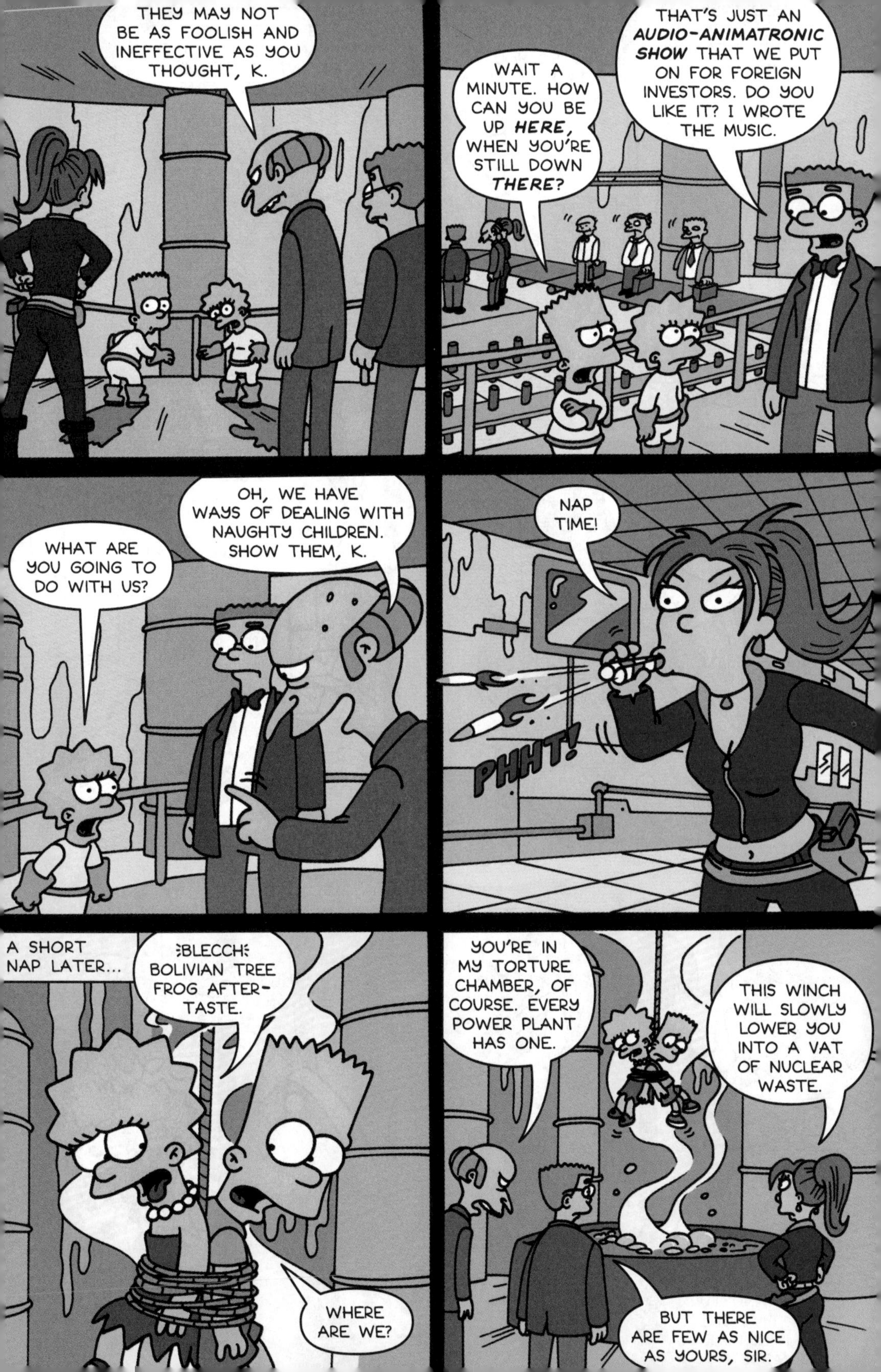
THEY MAY NOT BE AS FOOLISH AND INEFFECTIVE AS YOU THOUGHT, K.
WAIT A MINUTE. HOW CAN YOU BE UP HERE, WHEN YOU'RE STILL DOWN THERE?
THAT'S JUST AN AUDIO-ANIMATRONIC SHOW THAT WE PUT ON FOR FOREIGN INVESTORS. DO YOU LIKE IT? I WROTE THE MUSIC.
WHAT ARE YOU GOING TO DO WITH US?
OH, WE HAVE WAYS OF DEALING WITH NAUGHTY CHILDREN. SHOW THEM, K.
NAP TIME!
PHHT!
A SHORT NAP LATER...
BLECCH BOLIVIAN TREE FROG AFTER-TASTE.
WHERE ARE WE?
YOU'RE IN MY TORTURE CHAMBER, OF COURSE. EVERY POWER PLANT HAS ONE.
THIS WINCH WILL SLOWLY LOWER YOU INTO A VAT OF NUCLEAR WASTE.
BUT THERE ARE FEW AS NICE AS YOURS, SIR.

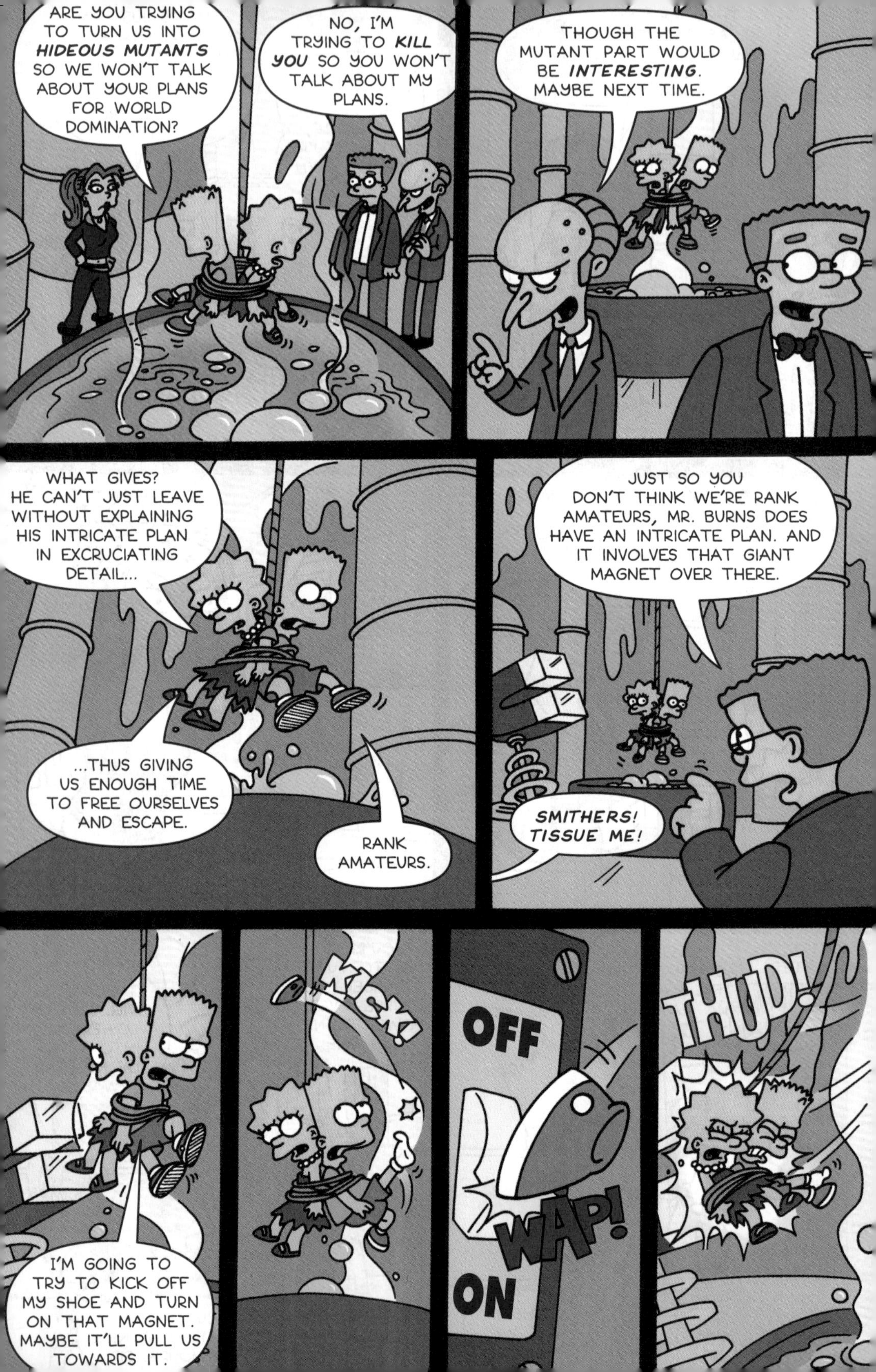
ARE YOU TRYING TO TURN US INTO HIDEOUS MUTANTS SO WE WON'T TALK ABOUT YOUR PLANS FOR WORLD DOMINATION?
NO, I'M TRYING TO KILL YOU SO YOU WON'T TALK ABOUT MY PLANS.
THOUGH THE MUTANT PART WOULD BE INTERESTING. MAYBE NEXT TIME.
WHAT GIVES? HE CAN'T JUST LEAVE WITHOUT EXPLAINING HIS INTRICATE PLAN IN EXCRUCIATING DETAIL...
...THUS GIVING US ENOUGH TIME TO FREE OURSELVES AND ESCAPE.
RANK AMATEURS.
JUST SO YOU DON'T THINK WE'RE RANK AMATEURS, MR. BURNS DOES HAVE AN INTRICATE PLAN. AND IT INVOLVES THAT GIANT MAGNET OVER THERE.
SMITHERS! TISSUE ME!
I'M GOING TO TRY TO KICK OFF MY SHOE AND TURN ON THAT MAGNET. MAYBE IT'LL PULL US TOWARDS IT.
KICK!
OFF
WAP!
ON
THUD!

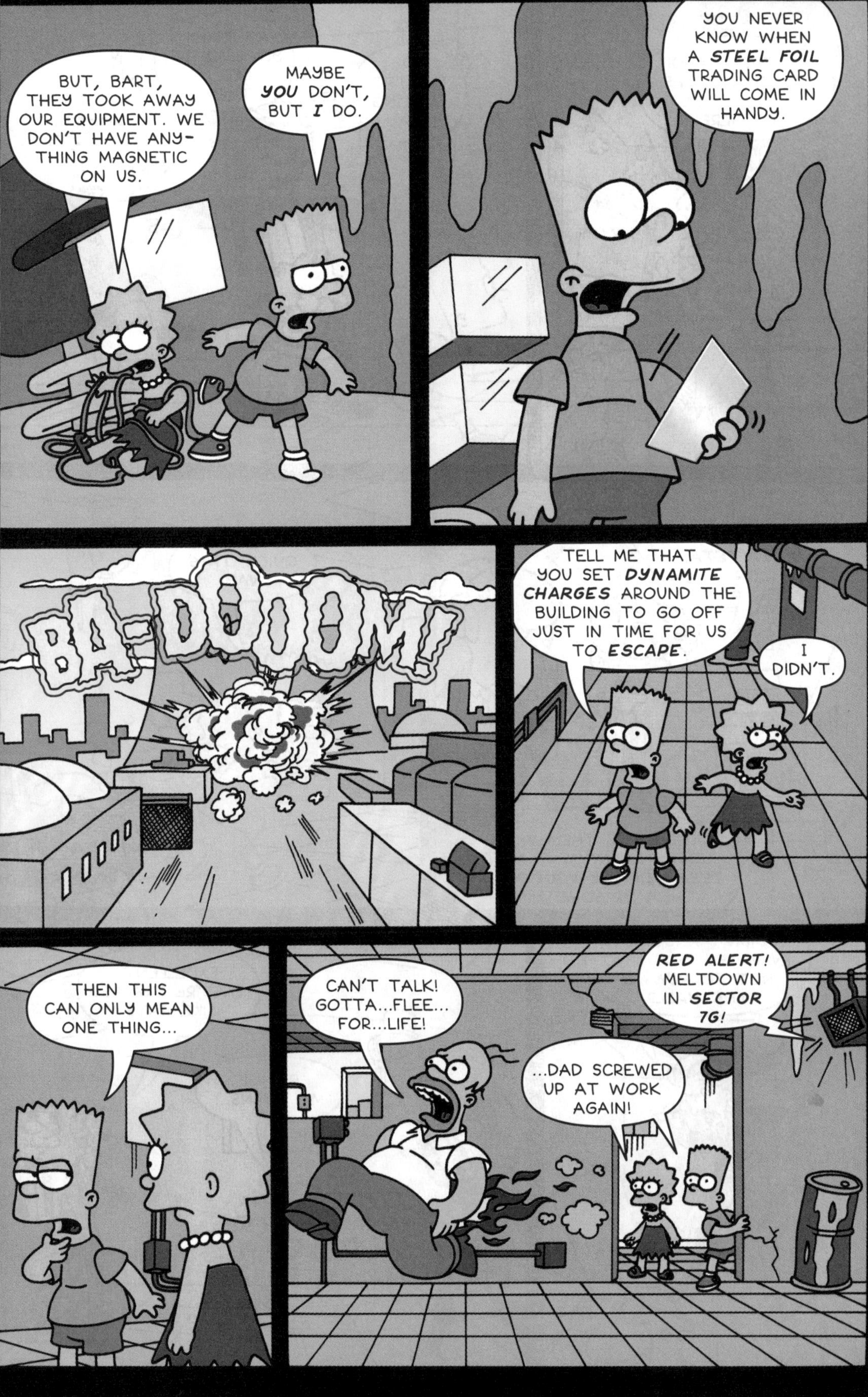
BUT, BART, THEY TOOK AWAY OUR EQUIPMENT. WE DON'T HAVE ANY-THING MAGNETIC ON US.
MAYBE YOU DON'T, BUT I DO.
YOU NEVER KNOW WHEN A STEEL FOIL TRADING CARD WILL COME IN HANDY.
BA-DOOOM!
TELL ME THAT YOU SET DYNAMITE CHARGES AROUND THE BUILDING TO GO OFF JUST IN TIME FOR US TO ESCAPE.
I DIDN'T.
THEN THIS CAN ONLY MEAN ONE THING...
CAN'T TALK! GOTTA...FLEE... FOR...LIFE!
RED ALERT! MELTDOWN IN SECTOR 7G!
...DAD SCREWED UP AT WORK AGAIN!

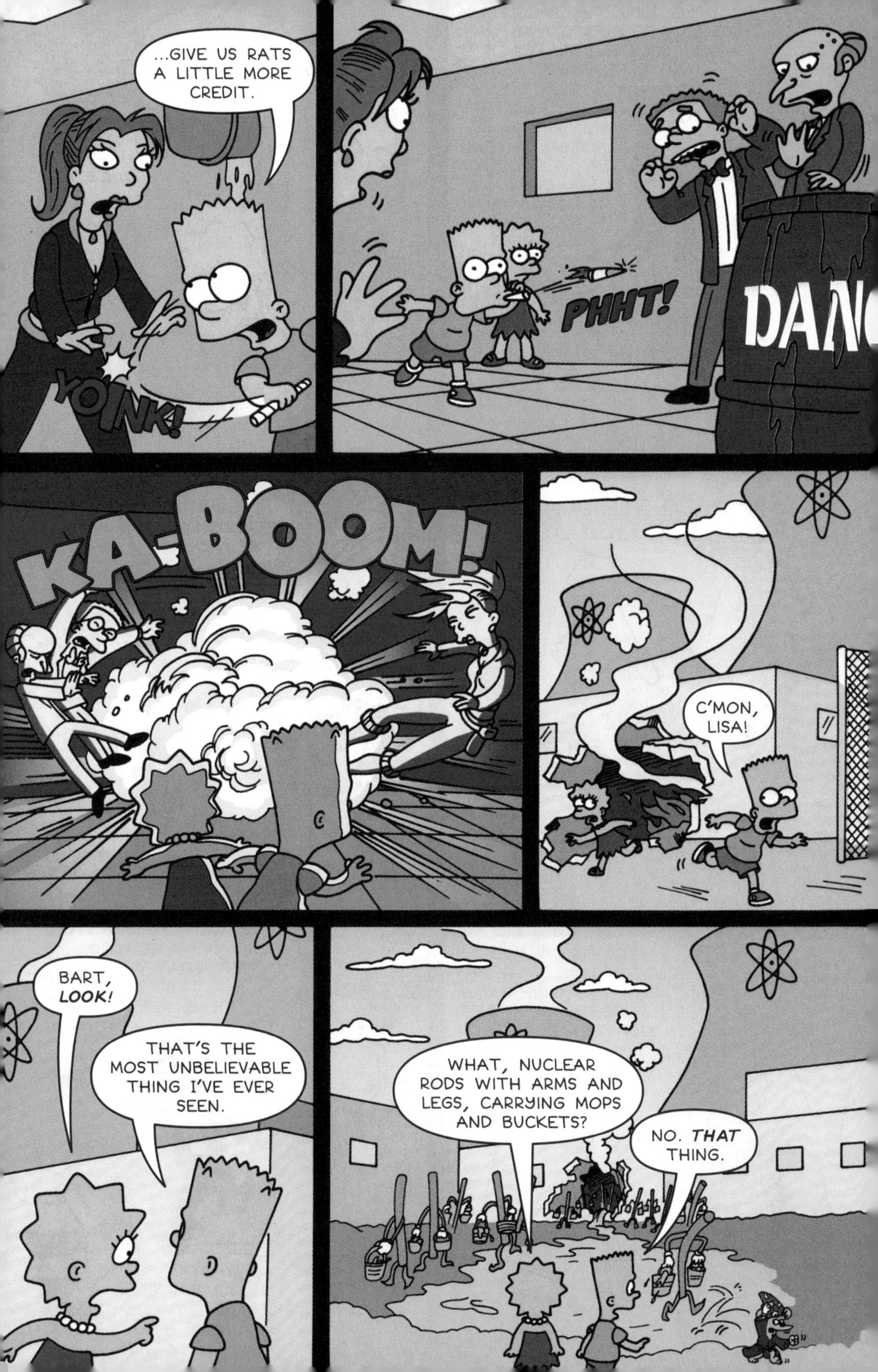
...GIVE US RATS A LITTLE MORE CREDIT.
YOINK!
PHHT!
DANG
KA-BOOM!
C'MON, LISA!
BART, **LOOK**!
THAT'S THE MOST UNBELIEVABLE THING I'VE EVER SEEN.
WHAT, NUCLEAR RODS WITH ARMS AND LEGS, CARRYING MOPS AND BUCKETS?
NO. ***THAT*** THING.

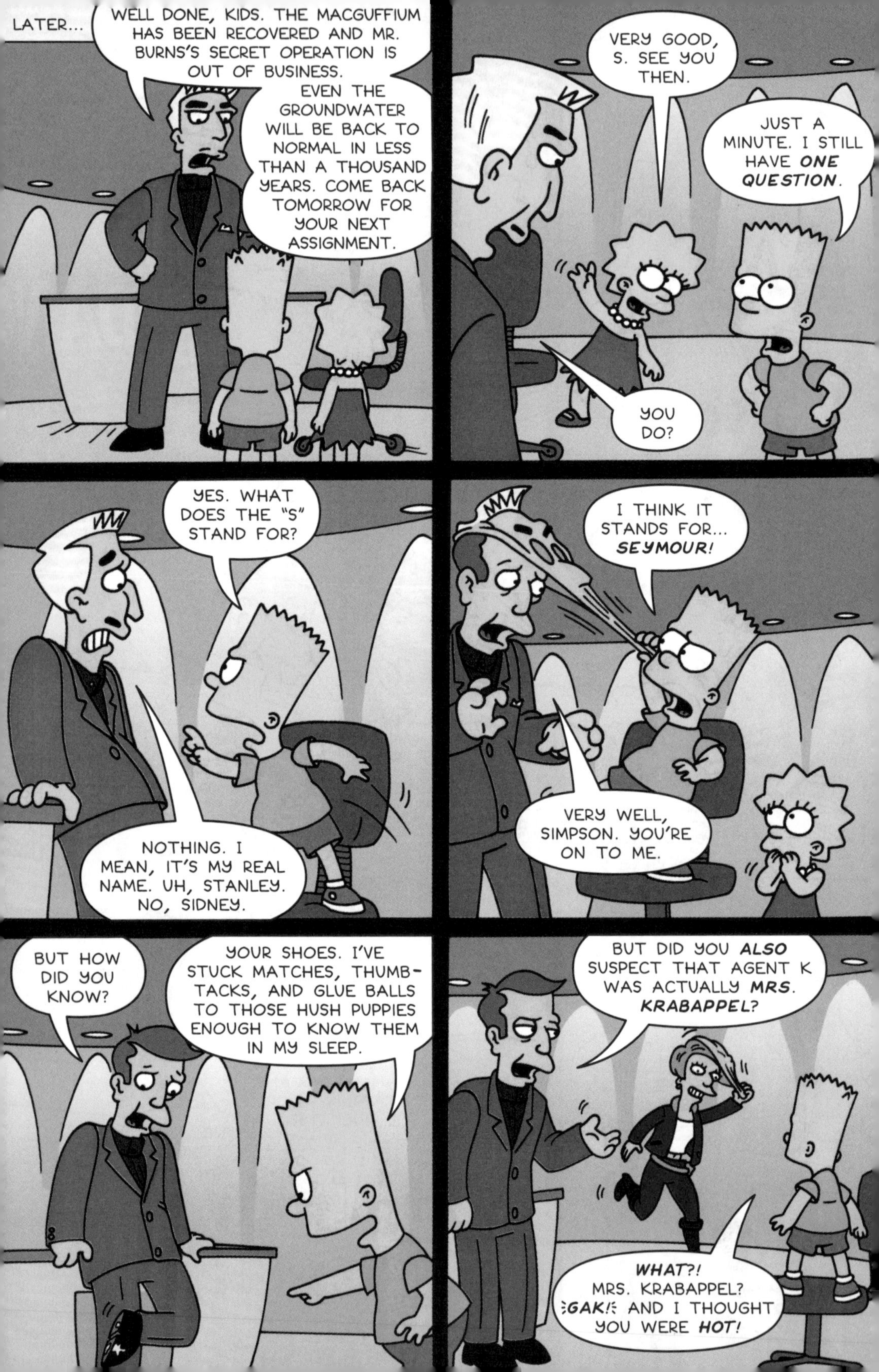
LATER...
WELL DONE, KIDS. THE MACGUFFIUM HAS BEEN RECOVERED AND MR. BURNS'S SECRET OPERATION IS OUT OF BUSINESS.
EVEN THE GROUNDWATER WILL BE BACK TO NORMAL IN LESS THAN A THOUSAND YEARS. COME BACK TOMORROW FOR YOUR NEXT ASSIGNMENT.
VERY GOOD, S. SEE YOU THEN.
JUST A MINUTE. I STILL HAVE **ONE QUESTION**.
YOU DO?
YES. WHAT DOES THE "S" STAND FOR?
NOTHING. I MEAN, IT'S MY REAL NAME. UH, STANLEY. NO, SIDNEY.
I THINK IT STANDS FOR... **SEYMOUR**!
VERY WELL, SIMPSON. YOU'RE ON TO ME.
BUT HOW DID YOU KNOW?
YOUR SHOES. I'VE STUCK MATCHES, THUMB-TACKS, AND GLUE BALLS TO THOSE HUSH PUPPIES ENOUGH TO KNOW THEM IN MY SLEEP.
BUT DID YOU **ALSO** SUSPECT THAT AGENT K WAS ACTUALLY **MRS. KRABAPPEL**?
WHAT?! MRS. KRABAPPEL? **GAK!** AND I THOUGHT YOU WERE **HOT**!

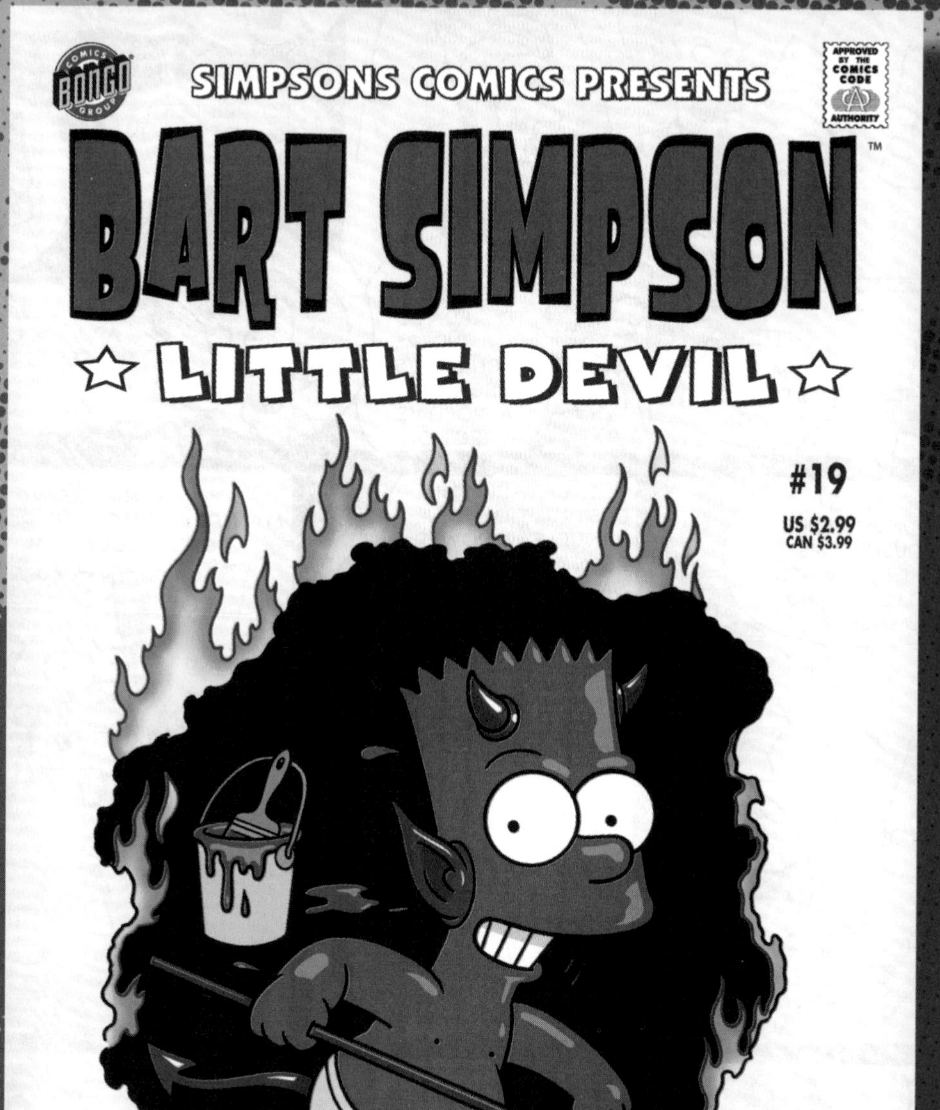
BONGO COMICS GROUP
SIMPSONS COMICS PRESENTS
APPROVED BY THE COMICS CODE AUTHORITY
BART SIMPSON™
LITTLE DEVIL
#19
US $2.99
CAN $3.99
MATT GROENING

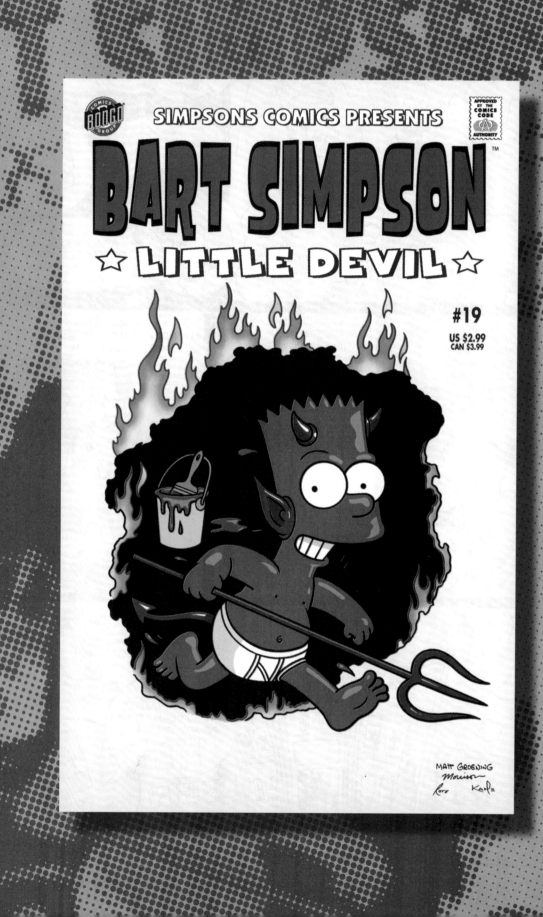

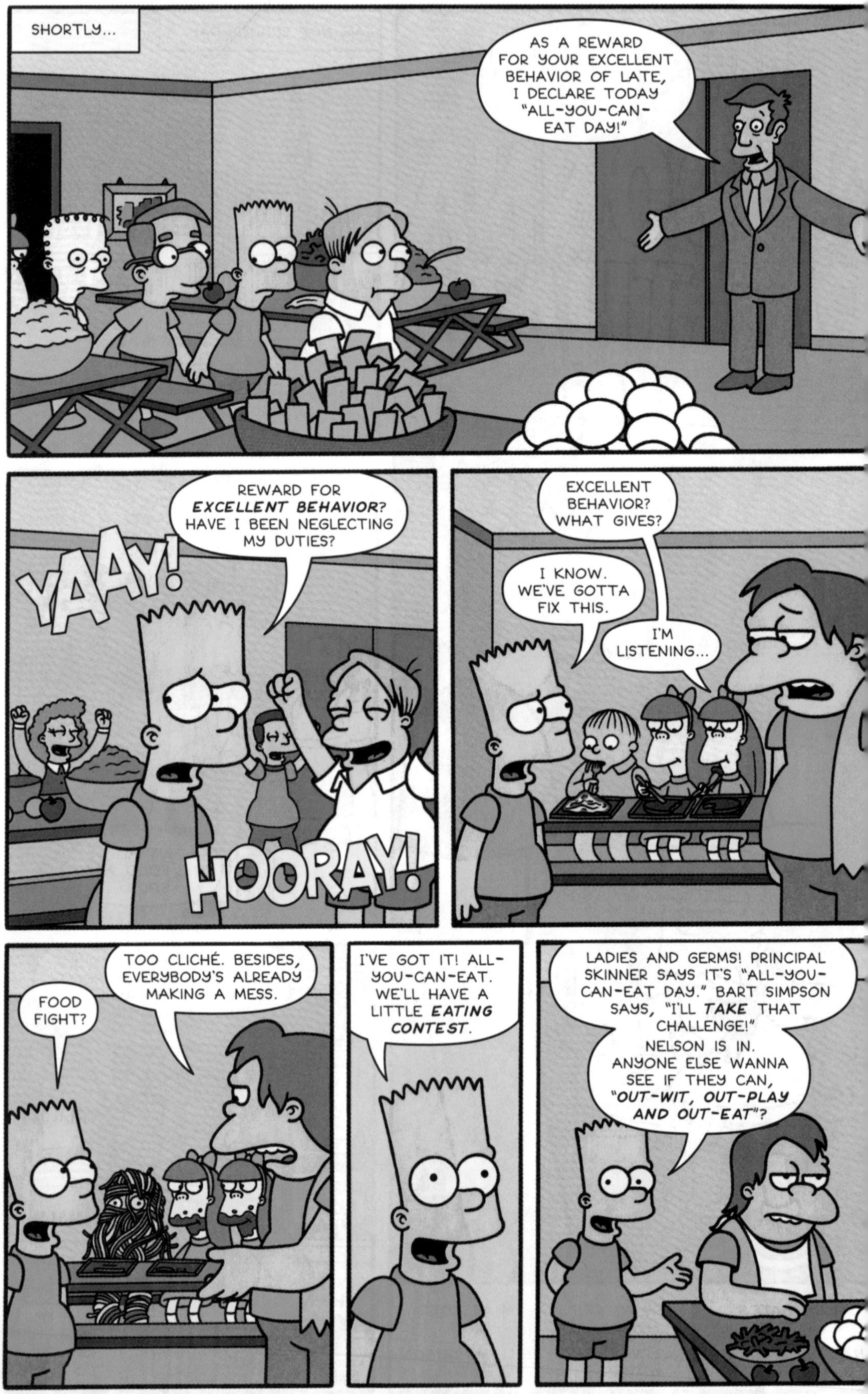

SHORTLY...
AS A REWARD FOR YOUR EXCELLENT BEHAVIOR OF LATE, I DECLARE TODAY "ALL-YOU-CAN-EAT DAY!"
REWARD FOR *EXCELLENT BEHAVIOR*? HAVE I BEEN NEGLECTING MY DUTIES?
YAAY!
HOORAY!
EXCELLENT BEHAVIOR? WHAT GIVES?
I KNOW. WE'VE GOTTA FIX THIS.
I'M LISTENING...
FOOD FIGHT?
TOO CLICHÉ. BESIDES, EVERYBODY'S ALREADY MAKING A MESS.
I'VE GOT IT! ALL-YOU-CAN-EAT. WE'LL HAVE A LITTLE *EATING CONTEST*.
LADIES AND GERMS! PRINCIPAL SKINNER SAYS IT'S "ALL-YOU-CAN-EAT DAY." BART SIMPSON SAYS, "I'LL *TAKE* THAT CHALLENGE!"
NELSON IS IN. ANYONE ELSE WANNA SEE IF THEY CAN, *"OUT-WIT, OUT-PLAY AND OUT-EAT"*?

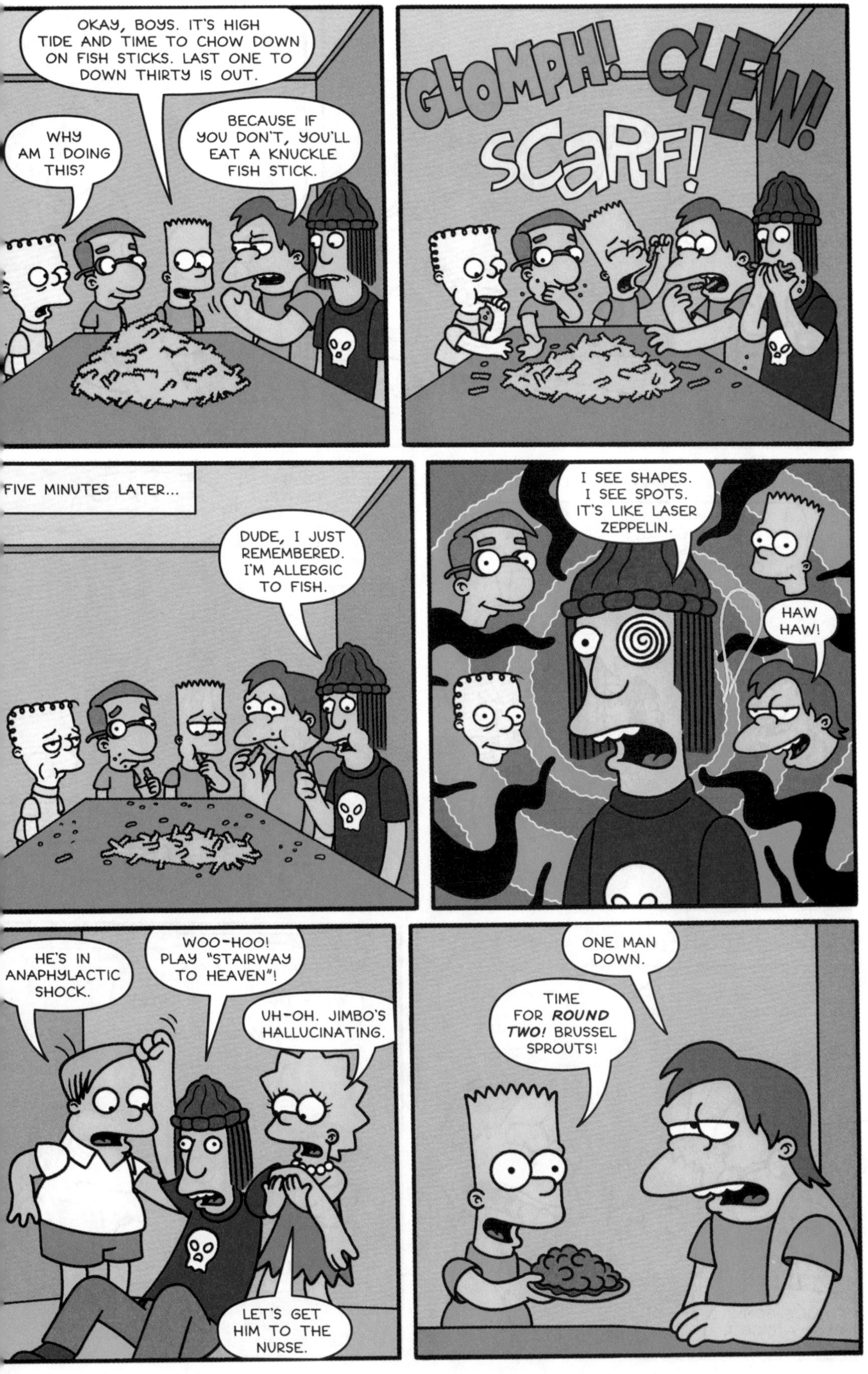
OKAY, BOYS. IT'S HIGH TIDE AND TIME TO CHOW DOWN ON FISH STICKS. LAST ONE TO DOWN THIRTY IS OUT.
WHY AM I DOING THIS?
BECAUSE IF YOU DON'T, YOU'LL EAT A KNUCKLE FISH STICK.
GLOMPH! CHEW!
SCARF!
FIVE MINUTES LATER...
DUDE, I JUST REMEMBERED. I'M ALLERGIC TO FISH.
I SEE SHAPES. I SEE SPOTS. IT'S LIKE LASER ZEPPELIN.
HAW HAW!
HE'S IN ANAPHYLACTIC SHOCK.
WOO-HOO! PLAY "STAIRWAY TO HEAVEN"!
UH-OH. JIMBO'S HALLUCINATING.
LET'S GET HIM TO THE NURSE.
ONE MAN DOWN.
TIME FOR ROUND TWO! BRUSSEL SPROUTS!

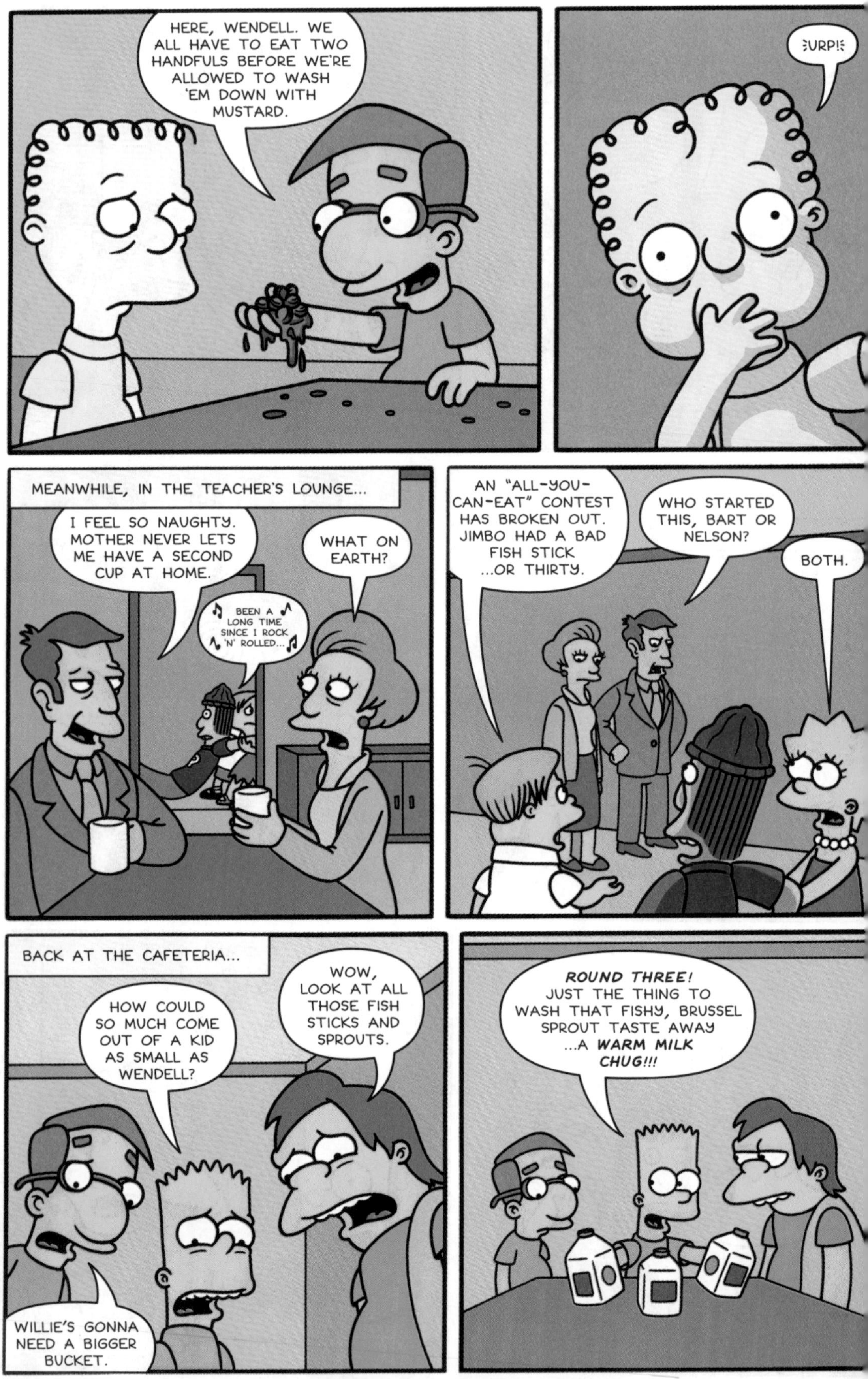

HERE, WENDELL. WE ALL HAVE TO EAT TWO HANDFULS BEFORE WE'RE ALLOWED TO WASH 'EM DOWN WITH MUSTARD.
URP!
MEANWHILE, IN THE TEACHER'S LOUNGE...
I FEEL SO NAUGHTY. MOTHER NEVER LETS ME HAVE A SECOND CUP AT HOME.
BEEN A LONG TIME SINCE I ROCK 'N' ROLLED...
WHAT ON EARTH?
AN "ALL-YOU-CAN-EAT" CONTEST HAS BROKEN OUT. JIMBO HAD A BAD FISH STICK ...OR THIRTY.
WHO STARTED THIS, BART OR NELSON?
BOTH.
BACK AT THE CAFETERIA...
HOW COULD SO MUCH COME OUT OF A KID AS SMALL AS WENDELL?
WOW, LOOK AT ALL THOSE FISH STICKS AND SPROUTS.
WILLIE'S GONNA NEED A BIGGER BUCKET.
ROUND THREE! JUST THE THING TO WASH THAT FISHY, BRUSSEL SPROUT TASTE AWAY ...A WARM MILK CHUG!!!

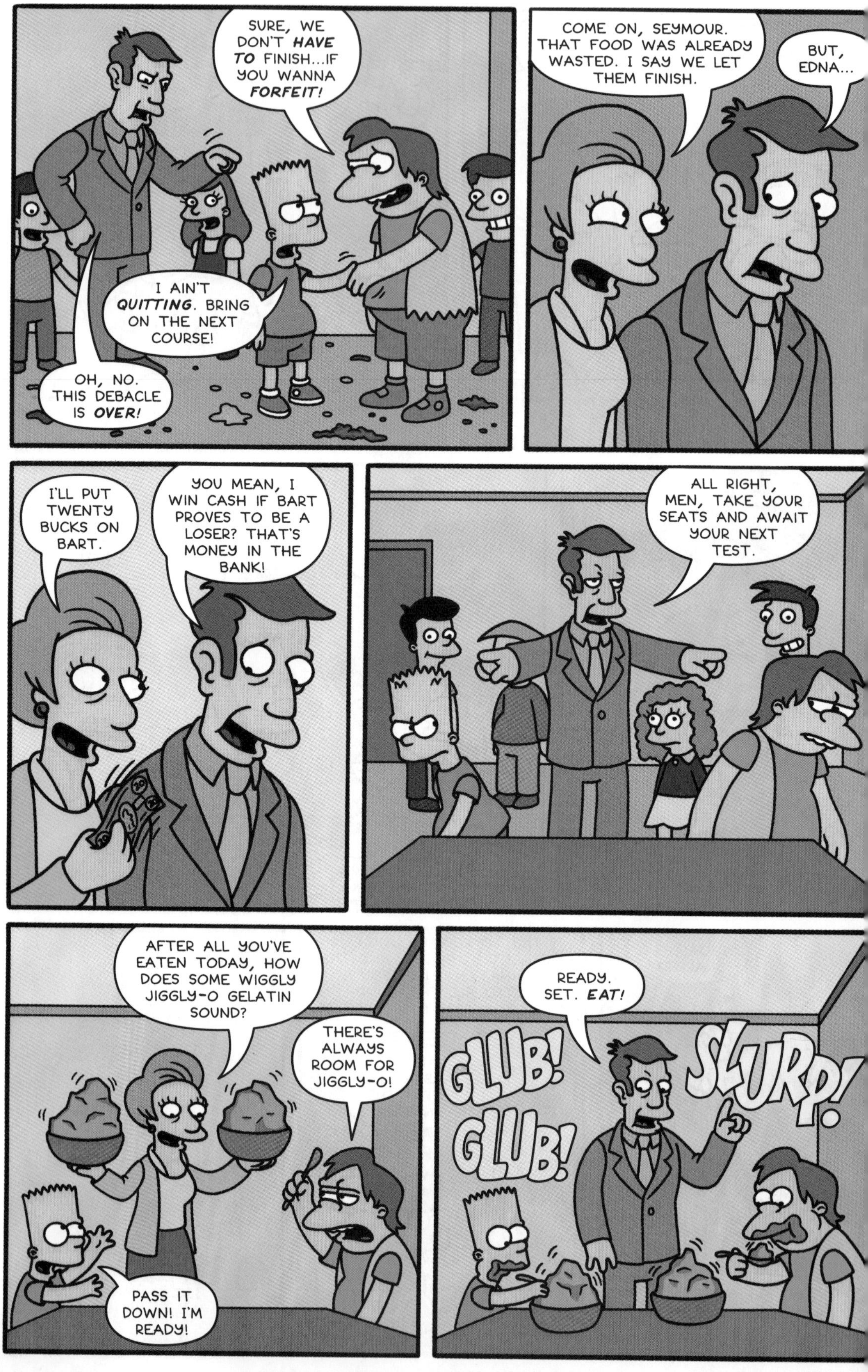
SURE, WE DON'T HAVE TO FINISH...IF YOU WANNA FORFEIT!
I AIN'T QUITTING. BRING ON THE NEXT COURSE!
OH, NO. THIS DEBACLE IS OVER!
COME ON, SEYMOUR. THAT FOOD WAS ALREADY WASTED. I SAY WE LET THEM FINISH.
BUT, EDNA...
I'LL PUT TWENTY BUCKS ON BART.
YOU MEAN, I WIN CASH IF BART PROVES TO BE A LOSER? THAT'S MONEY IN THE BANK!
ALL RIGHT, MEN, TAKE YOUR SEATS AND AWAIT YOUR NEXT TEST.
AFTER ALL YOU'VE EATEN TODAY, HOW DOES SOME WIGGLY JIGGLY-O GELATIN SOUND?
THERE'S ALWAYS ROOM FOR JIGGLY-O!
PASS IT DOWN! I'M READY!
READY. SET. EAT!
GLUB!
GLUB!
SLURP!

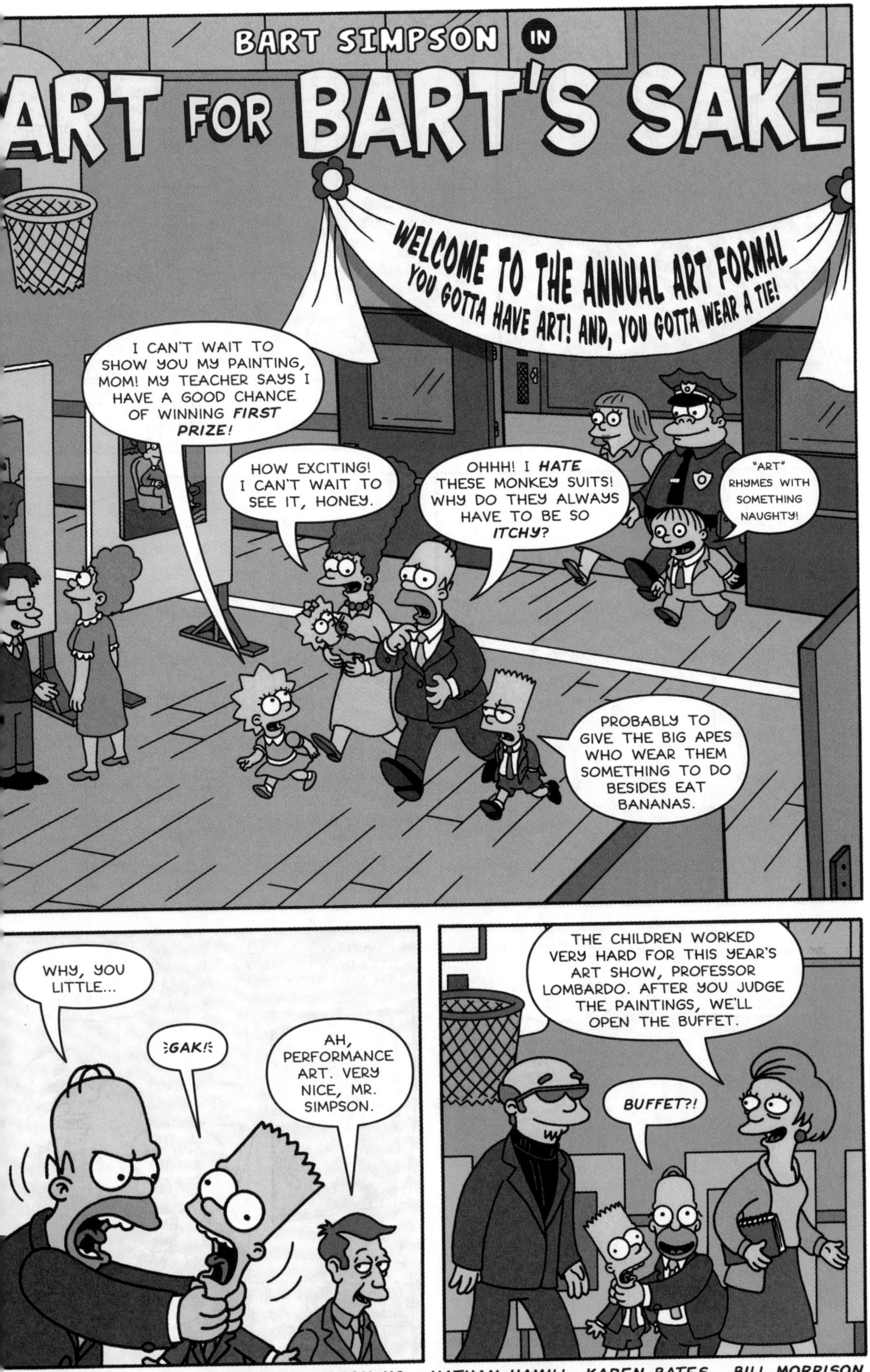
BART SIMPSON IN
ART FOR BART'S SAKE
WELCOME TO THE ANNUAL ART FORMAL
YOU GOTTA HAVE ART! AND, YOU GOTTA WEAR A TIE!
I CAN'T WAIT TO SHOW YOU MY PAINTING, MOM! MY TEACHER SAYS I HAVE A GOOD CHANCE OF WINNING *FIRST PRIZE!*
HOW EXCITING! I CAN'T WAIT TO SEE IT, HONEY.
OHHH! I *HATE* THESE MONKEY SUITS! WHY DO THEY ALWAYS HAVE TO BE SO *ITCHY?*
"ART" RHYMES WITH SOMETHING NAUGHTY!
PROBABLY TO GIVE THE BIG APES WHO WEAR THEM SOMETHING TO DO BESIDES EAT BANANAS.
WHY, YOU LITTLE...
GAK!
AH, PERFORMANCE ART. VERY NICE, MR. SIMPSON.
THE CHILDREN WORKED VERY HARD FOR THIS YEAR'S ART SHOW, PROFESSOR LOMBARDO. AFTER YOU JUDGE THE PAINTINGS, WE'LL OPEN THE BUFFET.
BUFFET?!

CHRIS YAMBAR WRITER · *MIKE KAZALEH* PENCILS · *JASON HO* INKS · *NATHAN HAMILL* COLORS · *KAREN BATES* LETTERS · *BILL MORRISON* EDITOR

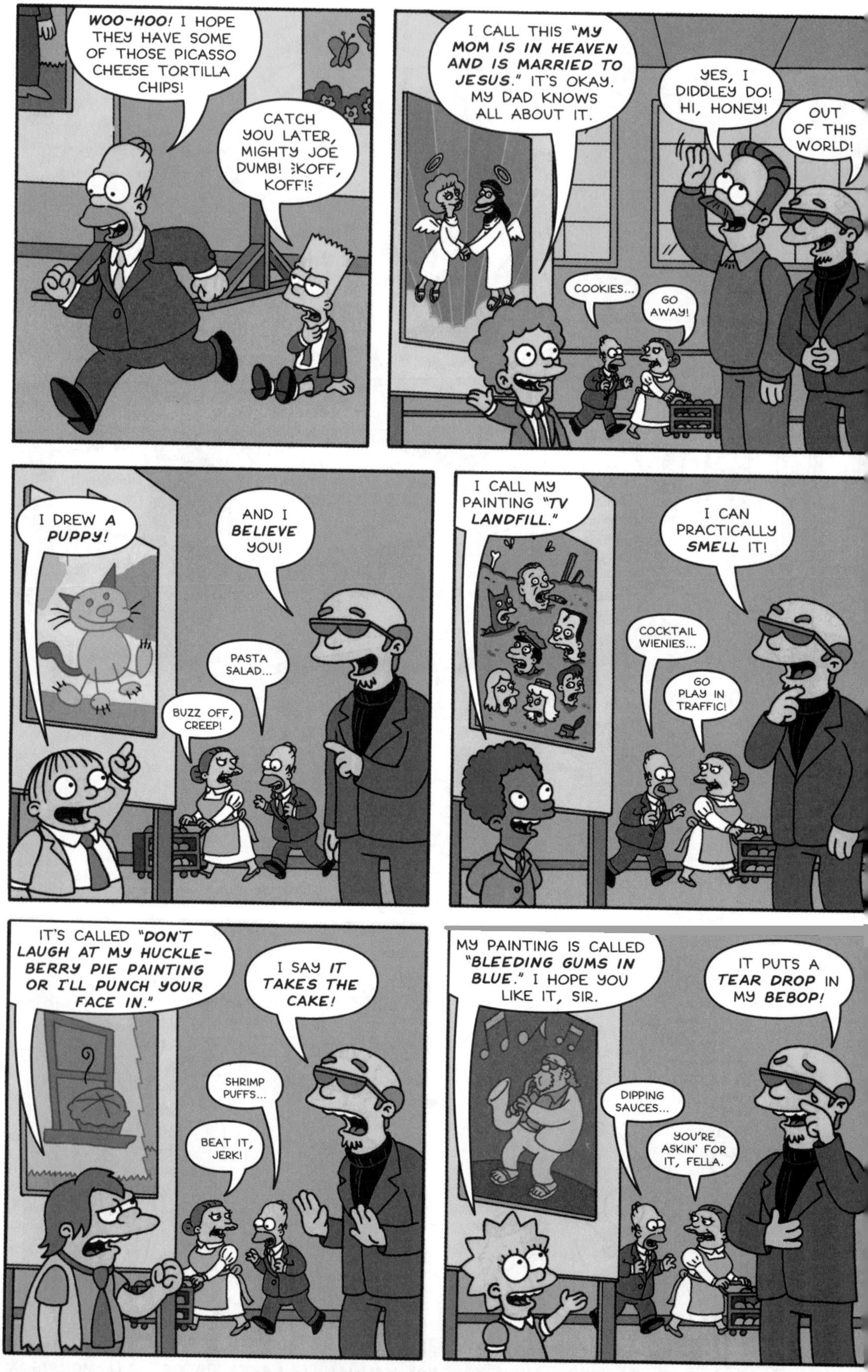

WOO-HOO! I HOPE THEY HAVE SOME OF THOSE PICASSO CHEESE TORTILLA CHIPS!
CATCH YOU LATER, MIGHTY JOE DUMB! KOFF, KOFF!
I CALL THIS "MY MOM IS IN HEAVEN AND IS MARRIED TO JESUS." IT'S OKAY. MY DAD KNOWS ALL ABOUT IT.
YES, I DIDDLEY DO! HI, HONEY!
OUT OF THIS WORLD!
COOKIES...
GO AWAY!
I DREW A PUPPY!
AND I BELIEVE YOU!
PASTA SALAD...
BUZZ OFF, CREEP!
I CALL MY PAINTING "TV LANDFILL."
I CAN PRACTICALLY SMELL IT!
COCKTAIL WIENIES...
GO PLAY IN TRAFFIC!
IT'S CALLED "DON'T LAUGH AT MY HUCKLEBERRY PIE PAINTING OR I'LL PUNCH YOUR FACE IN."
I SAY IT TAKES THE CAKE!
SHRIMP PUFFS...
BEAT IT, JERK!
MY PAINTING IS CALLED "BLEEDING GUMS IN BLUE." I HOPE YOU LIKE IT, SIR.
IT PUTS A TEAR DROP IN MY BEBOP!
DIPPING SAUCES...
YOU'RE ASKIN' FOR IT, FELLA.

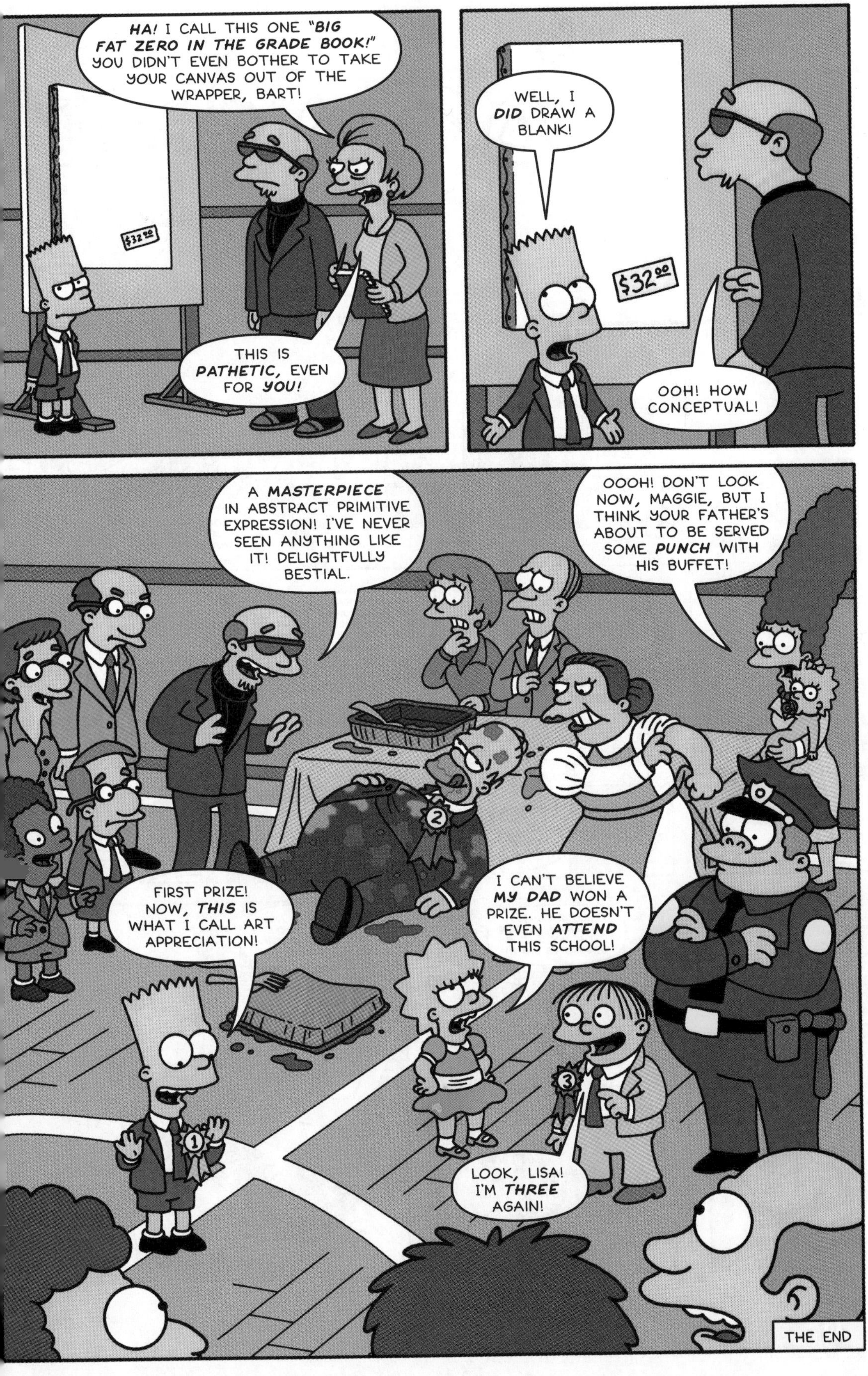

HA! I CALL THIS ONE "BIG FAT ZERO IN THE GRADE BOOK!" YOU DIDN'T EVEN BOTHER TO TAKE YOUR CANVAS OUT OF THE WRAPPER, BART!
$32.00
THIS IS PATHETIC, EVEN FOR YOU!
WELL, I DID DRAW A BLANK!
$32.00
OOH! HOW CONCEPTUAL!
A MASTERPIECE IN ABSTRACT PRIMITIVE EXPRESSION! I'VE NEVER SEEN ANYTHING LIKE IT! DELIGHTFULLY BESTIAL.
OOOH! DON'T LOOK NOW, MAGGIE, BUT I THINK YOUR FATHER'S ABOUT TO BE SERVED SOME PUNCH WITH HIS BUFFET!
FIRST PRIZE! NOW, THIS IS WHAT I CALL ART APPRECIATION!
I CAN'T BELIEVE MY DAD WON A PRIZE. HE DOESN'T EVEN ATTEND THIS SCHOOL!
LOOK, LISA! I'M THREE AGAIN!
THE END

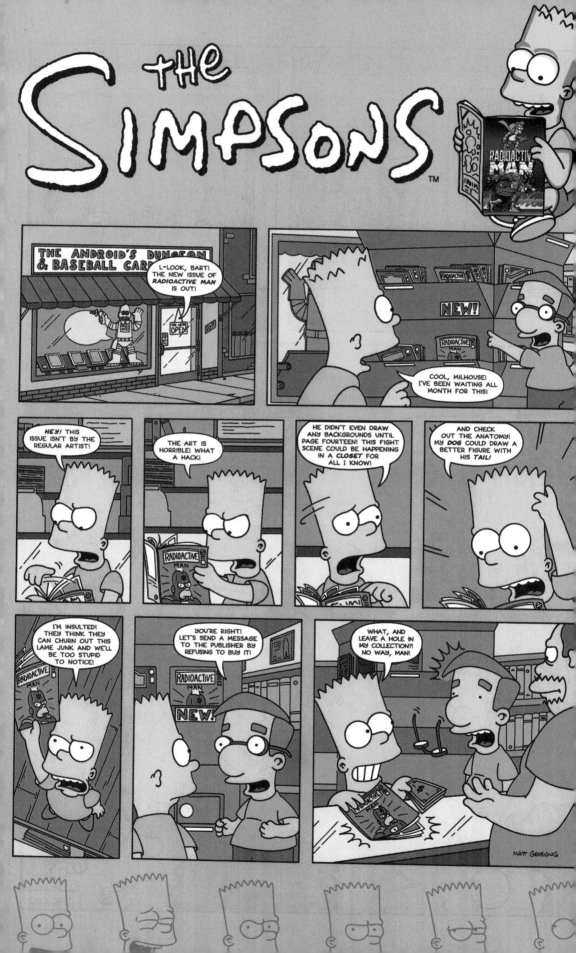

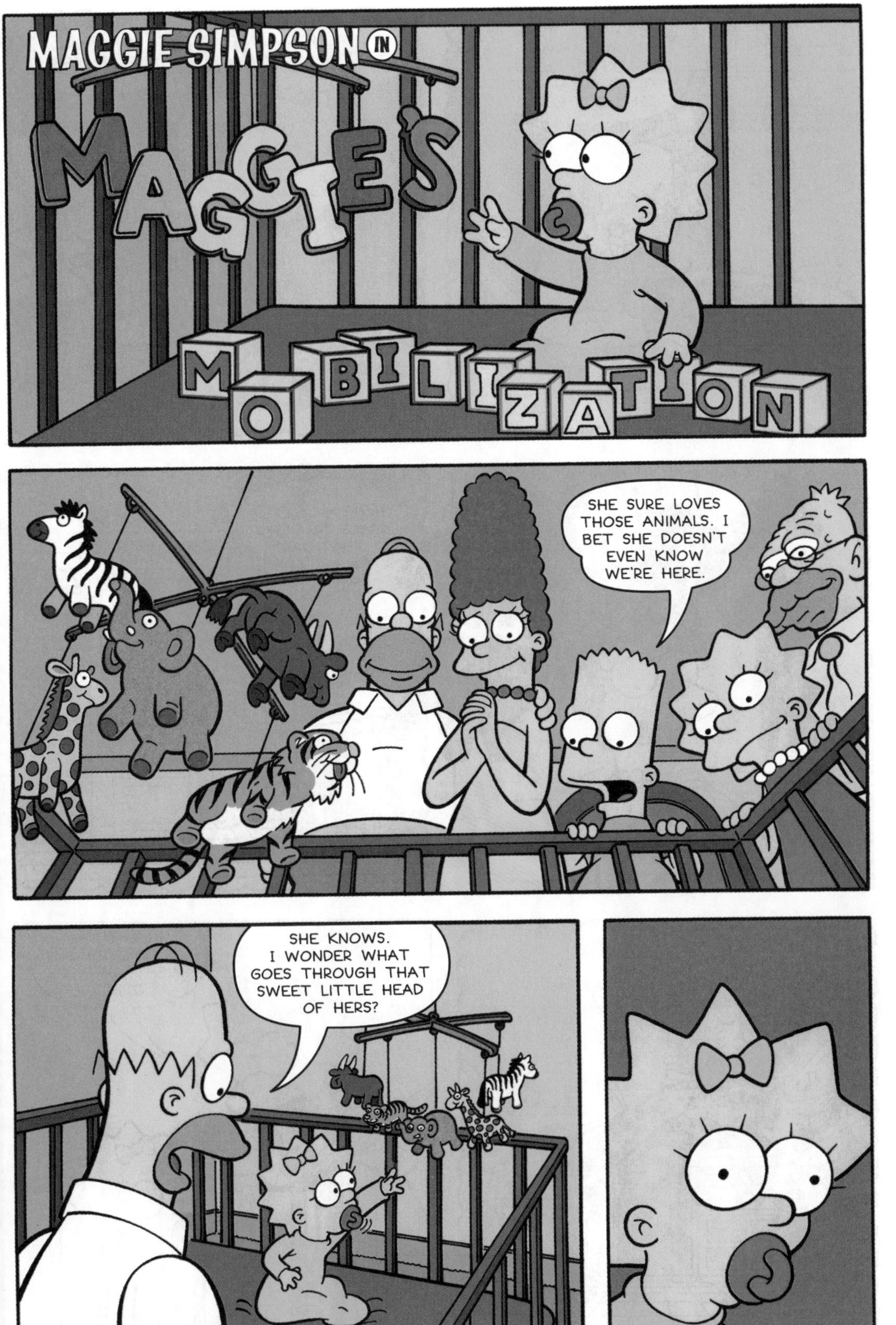
MAGGIE SIMPSON IN
MAGGIE'S
MOBILIZATION
SHE SURE LOVES THOSE ANIMALS. I BET SHE DOESN'T EVEN KNOW WE'RE HERE.
SHE KNOWS. I WONDER WHAT GOES THROUGH THAT SWEET LITTLE HEAD OF HERS?

JAMES BATES WRITER · MARK ERVIN PENCILS · MIKE DECARLO INKS · NATHAN HAMILL COLORS · KAREN BATES LETTERS · BILL MORRISON EDITOR

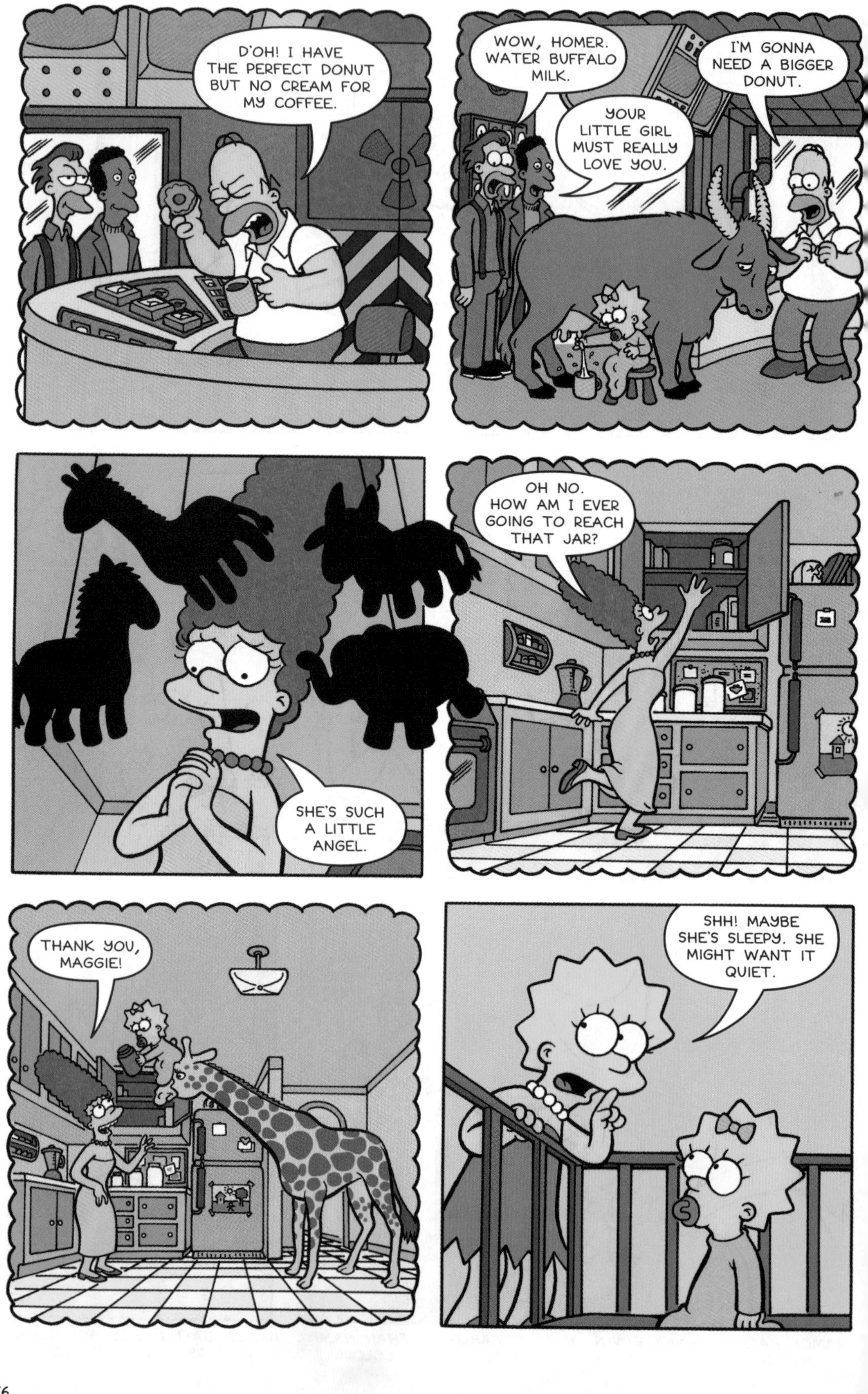
D'OH! I HAVE THE PERFECT DONUT BUT NO CREAM FOR MY COFFEE.
WOW, HOMER. WATER BUFFALO MILK.
YOUR LITTLE GIRL MUST REALLY LOVE YOU.
I'M GONNA NEED A BIGGER DONUT.
SHE'S SUCH A LITTLE ANGEL.
OH NO. HOW AM I EVER GOING TO REACH THAT JAR?
THANK YOU, MAGGIE!
SHH! MAYBE SHE'S SLEEPY. SHE MIGHT WANT IT QUIET.

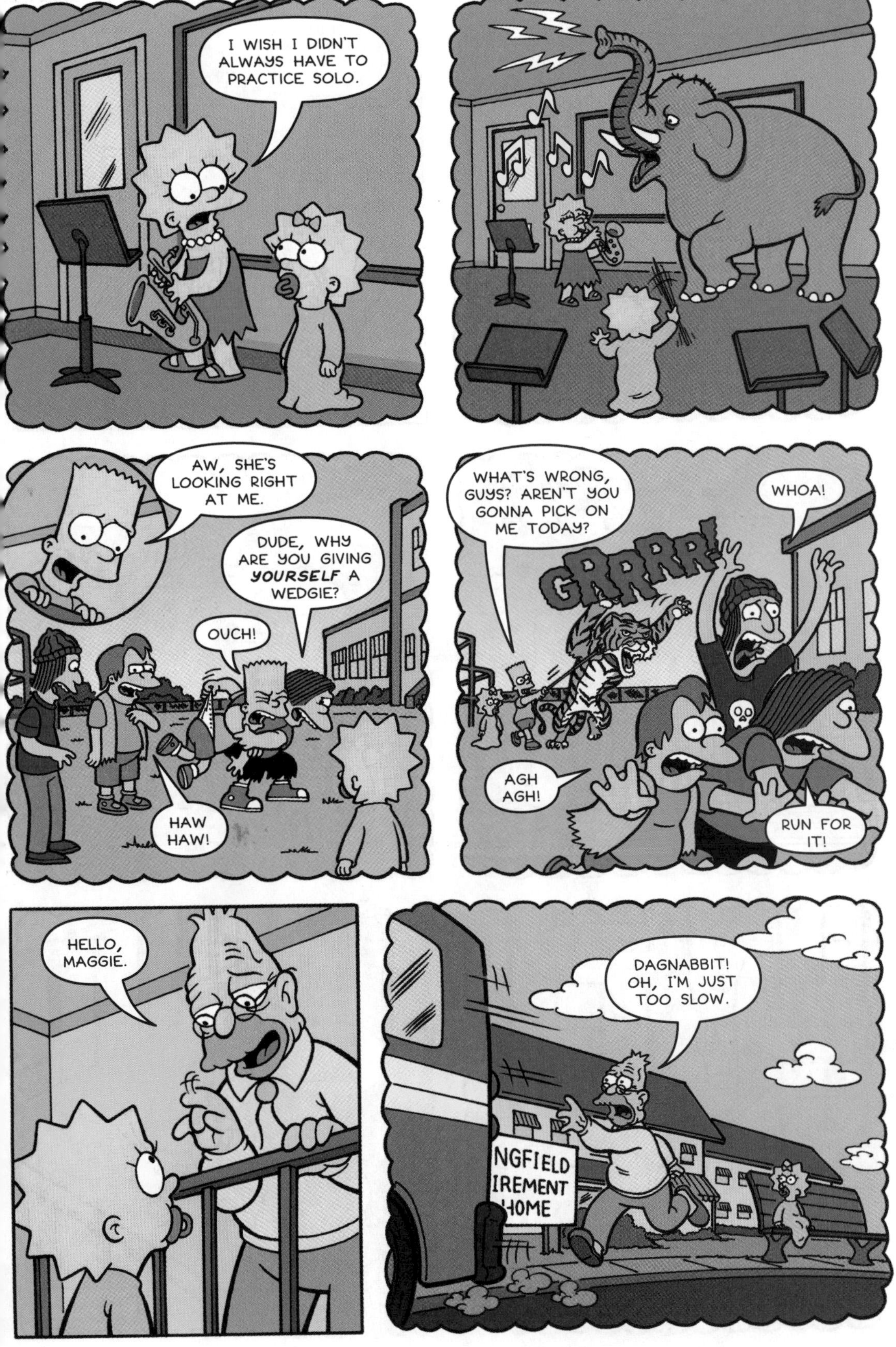
I WISH I DIDN'T ALWAYS HAVE TO PRACTICE SOLO.
AW, SHE'S LOOKING RIGHT AT ME.
DUDE, WHY ARE YOU GIVING *YOURSELF* A WEDGIE?
OUCH!
HAW HAW!
WHAT'S WRONG, GUYS? AREN'T YOU GONNA PICK ON ME TODAY?
WHOA!
GRRRR!
AGH AGH!
RUN FOR IT!
HELLO, MAGGIE.
DAGNABBIT! OH, I'M JUST TOO SLOW.
NGFIELD
IREMENT
HOME

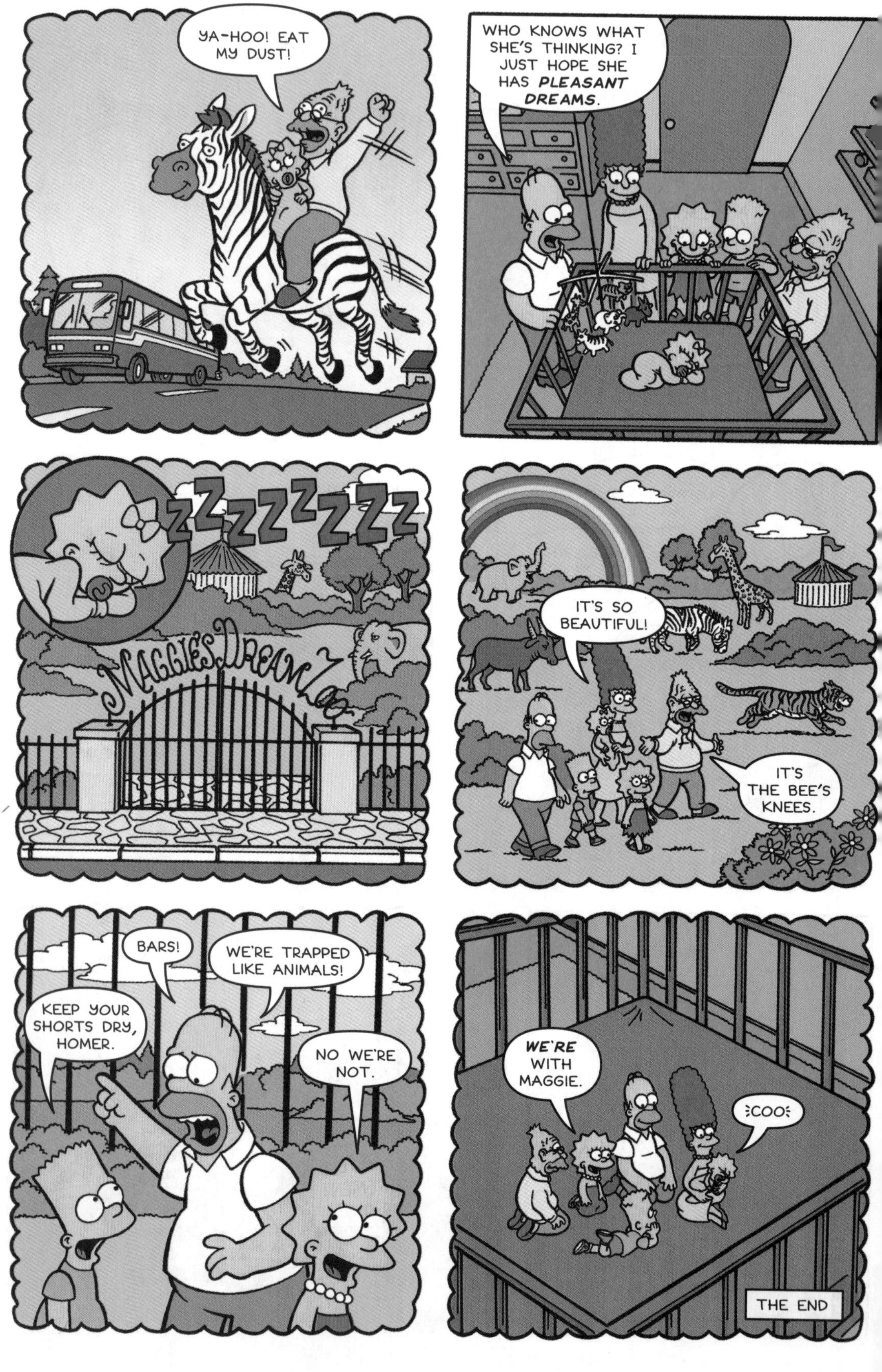

YA-HOO! EAT MY DUST!
WHO KNOWS WHAT SHE'S THINKING? I JUST HOPE SHE HAS **PLEASANT DREAMS**.
ZZZZZZZZZ
MAGGIE'S DREAM ZOO
IT'S SO BEAUTIFUL!
IT'S THE BEE'S KNEES.
BARS!
WE'RE TRAPPED LIKE ANIMALS!
KEEP YOUR SHORTS DRY, HOMER.
NO WE'RE NOT.
WE'RE WITH MAGGIE.
COO
THE END

THE MEDIOCRE MISADVENTURES OF MARTIN & MILHOUSE!
BARTLESS ON A TUESDAY

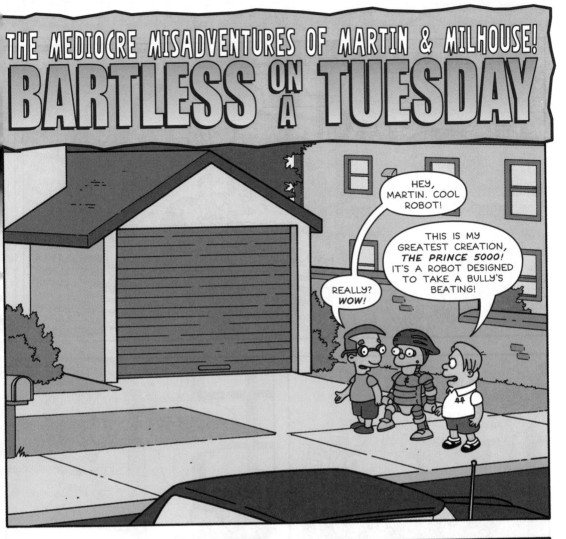

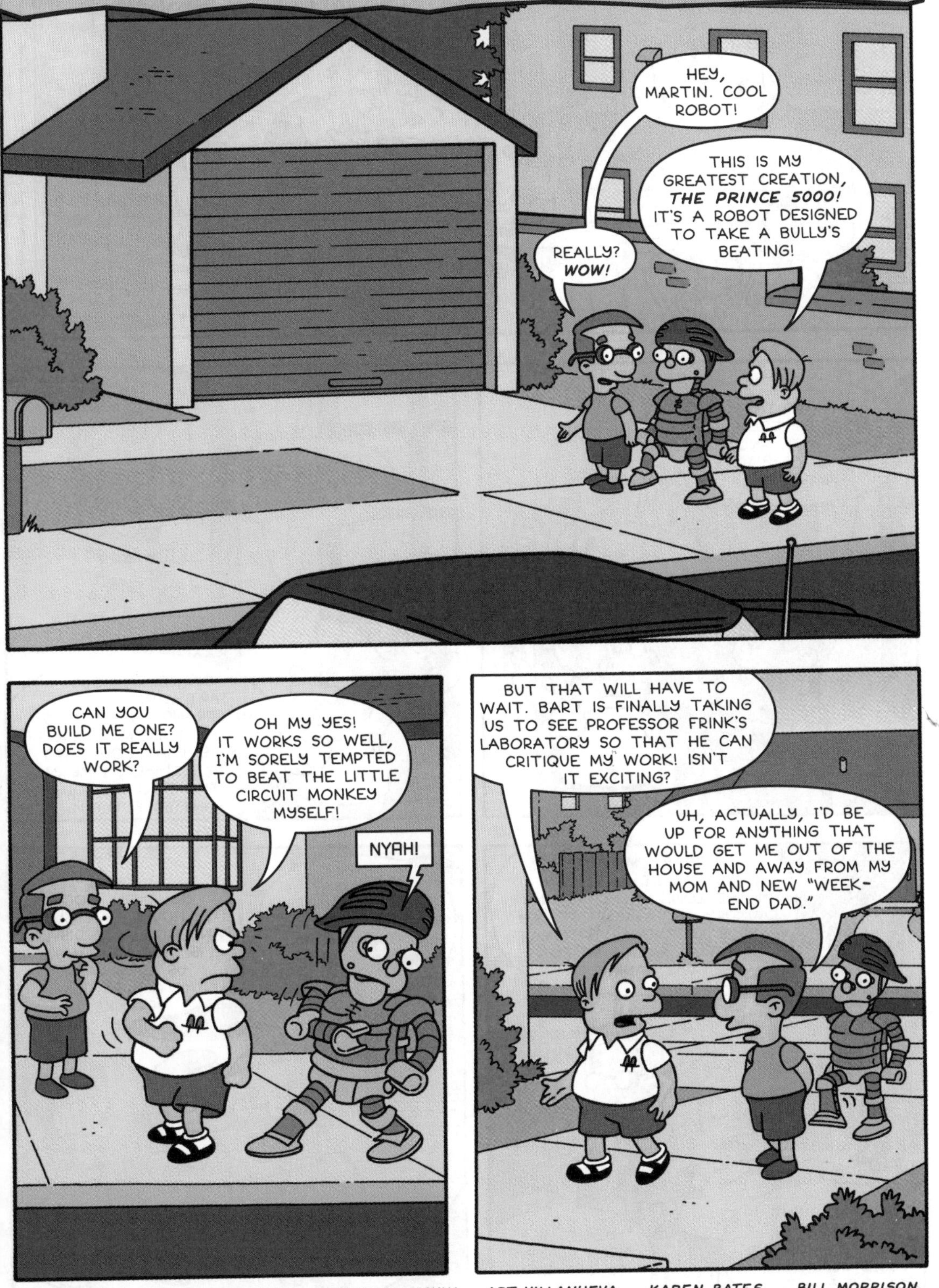
HEY, MARTIN. COOL ROBOT!
THIS IS MY GREATEST CREATION, ***THE PRINCE 5000!*** IT'S A ROBOT DESIGNED TO TAKE A BULLY'S BEATING!
REALLY? ***WOW!***
CAN YOU BUILD ME ONE? DOES IT REALLY WORK?
OH MY YES! IT WORKS SO WELL, I'M SORELY TEMPTED TO BEAT THE LITTLE CIRCUIT MONKEY MYSELF!
NYAH!
BUT THAT WILL HAVE TO WAIT. BART IS FINALLY TAKING US TO SEE PROFESSOR FRINK'S LABORATORY SO THAT HE CAN CRITIQUE MY WORK! ISN'T IT EXCITING?
UH, ACTUALLY, I'D BE UP FOR ANYTHING THAT WOULD GET ME OUT OF THE HOUSE AND AWAY FROM MY MOM AND NEW "WEEK-END DAD."

TONY DIGEROLAMO WRITER ***JOHN COSTANZA*** PENCILS ***PHYLLIS NOVIN*** INKS ***ART VILLANUEVA*** COLORS ***KAREN BATES*** LETTERS ***BILL MORRISON*** EDITOR

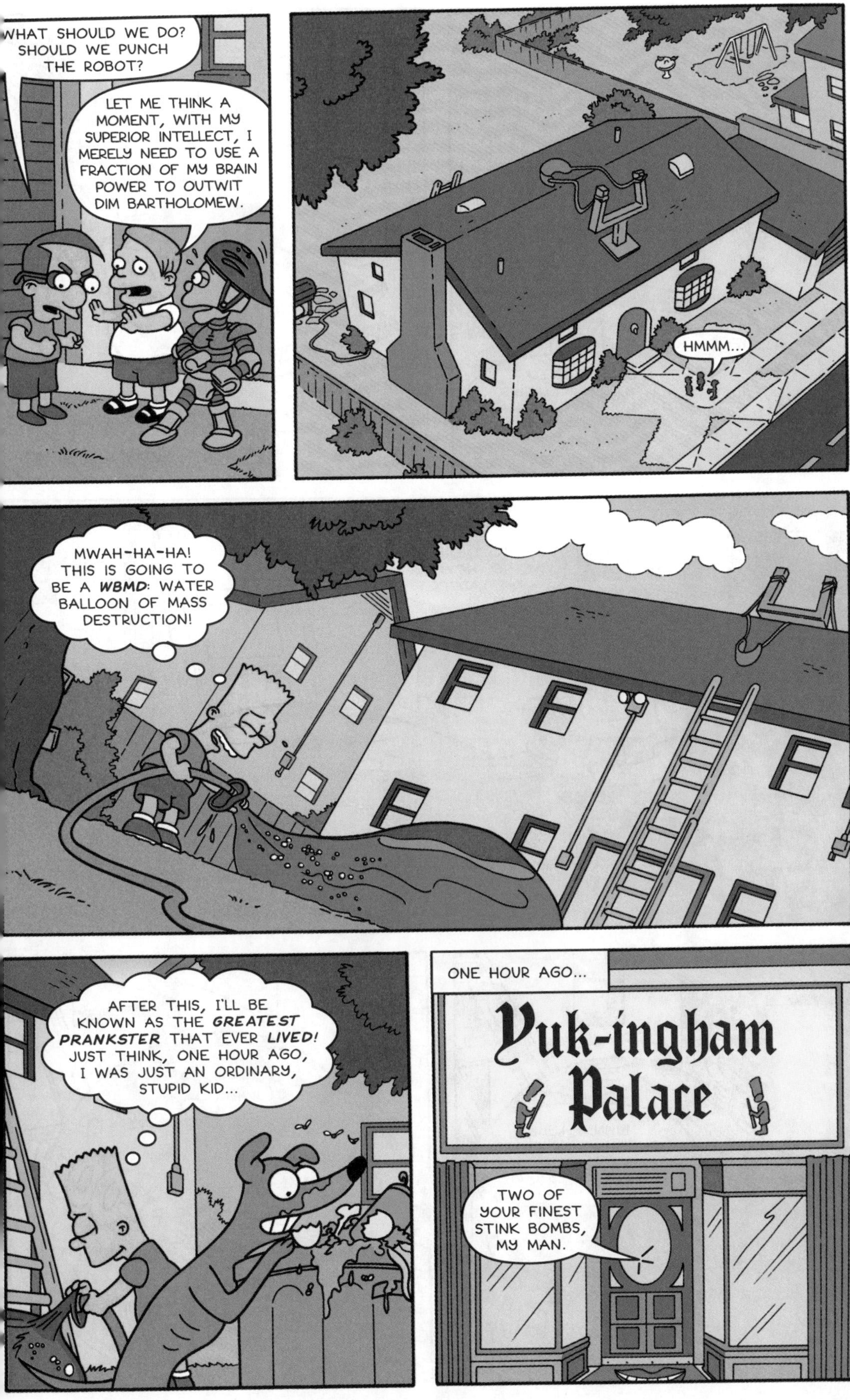

WHAT SHOULD WE DO? SHOULD WE PUNCH THE ROBOT?
LET ME THINK A MOMENT, WITH MY SUPERIOR INTELLECT, I MERELY NEED TO USE A FRACTION OF MY BRAIN POWER TO OUTWIT DIM BARTHOLOMEW.
HMMM...
MWAH-HA-HA! THIS IS GOING TO BE A **WBMD**: WATER BALLOON OF MASS DESTRUCTION!
AFTER THIS, I'LL BE KNOWN AS THE ***GREATEST PRANKSTER*** THAT EVER ***LIVED***! JUST THINK, ONE HOUR AGO, I WAS JUST AN ORDINARY, STUPID KID...
ONE HOUR AGO...
Yuk-ingham Palace
TWO OF YOUR FINEST STINK BOMBS, MY MAN.

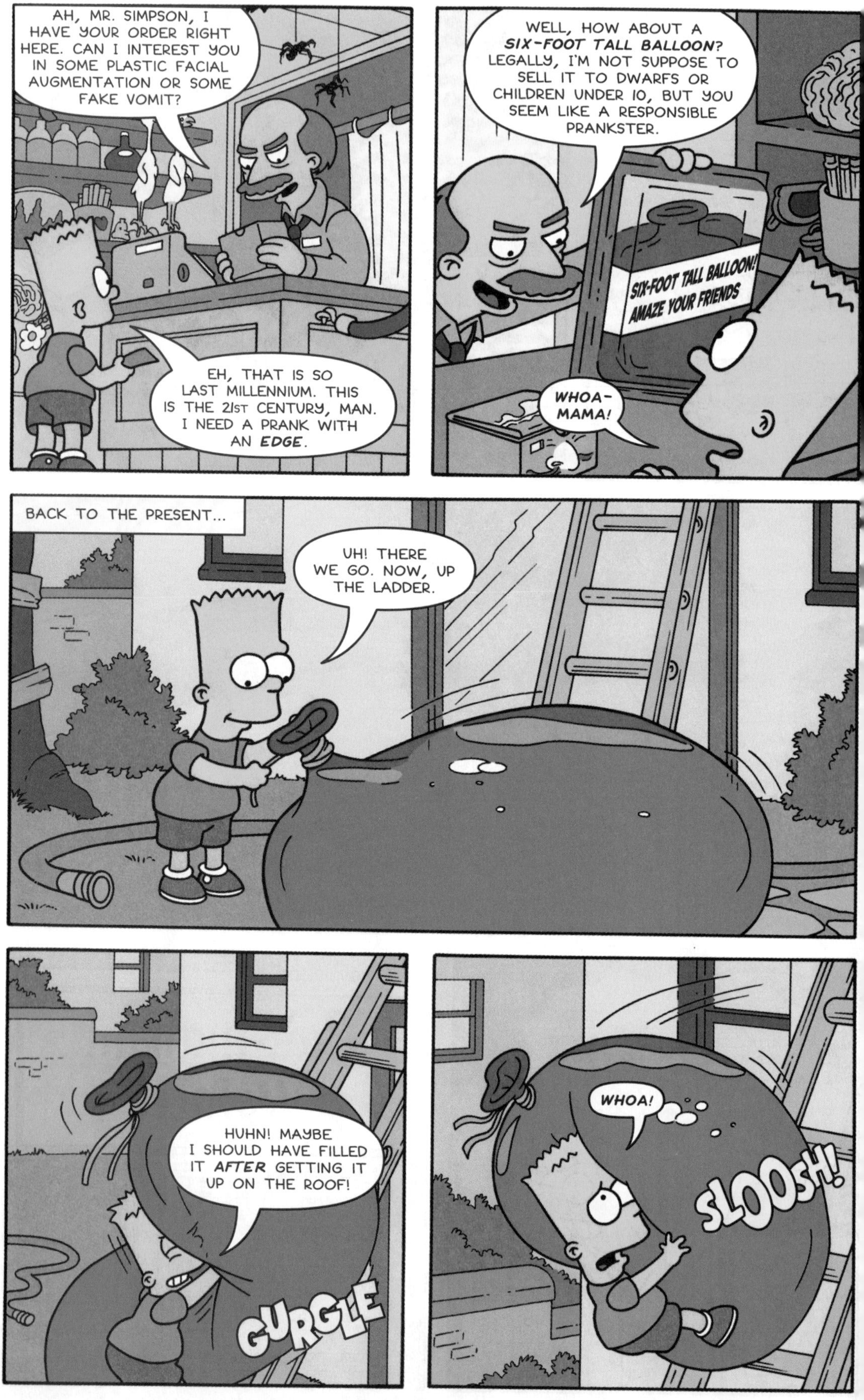
AH, MR. SIMPSON, I HAVE YOUR ORDER RIGHT HERE. CAN I INTEREST YOU IN SOME PLASTIC FACIAL AUGMENTATION OR SOME FAKE VOMIT?
EH, THAT IS SO LAST MILLENNIUM. THIS IS THE 21ST CENTURY, MAN. I NEED A PRANK WITH AN EDGE.
WELL, HOW ABOUT A SIX-FOOT TALL BALLOON? LEGALLY, I'M NOT SUPPOSE TO SELL IT TO DWARFS OR CHILDREN UNDER 10, BUT YOU SEEM LIKE A RESPONSIBLE PRANKSTER.
SIX-FOOT TALL BALLOON! AMAZE YOUR FRIENDS
WHOA-MAMA!
BACK TO THE PRESENT...
UH! THERE WE GO. NOW, UP THE LADDER.
HUHN! MAYBE I SHOULD HAVE FILLED IT AFTER GETTING IT UP ON THE ROOF!
GURGLE
WHOA!
SLOOSH!

83

84

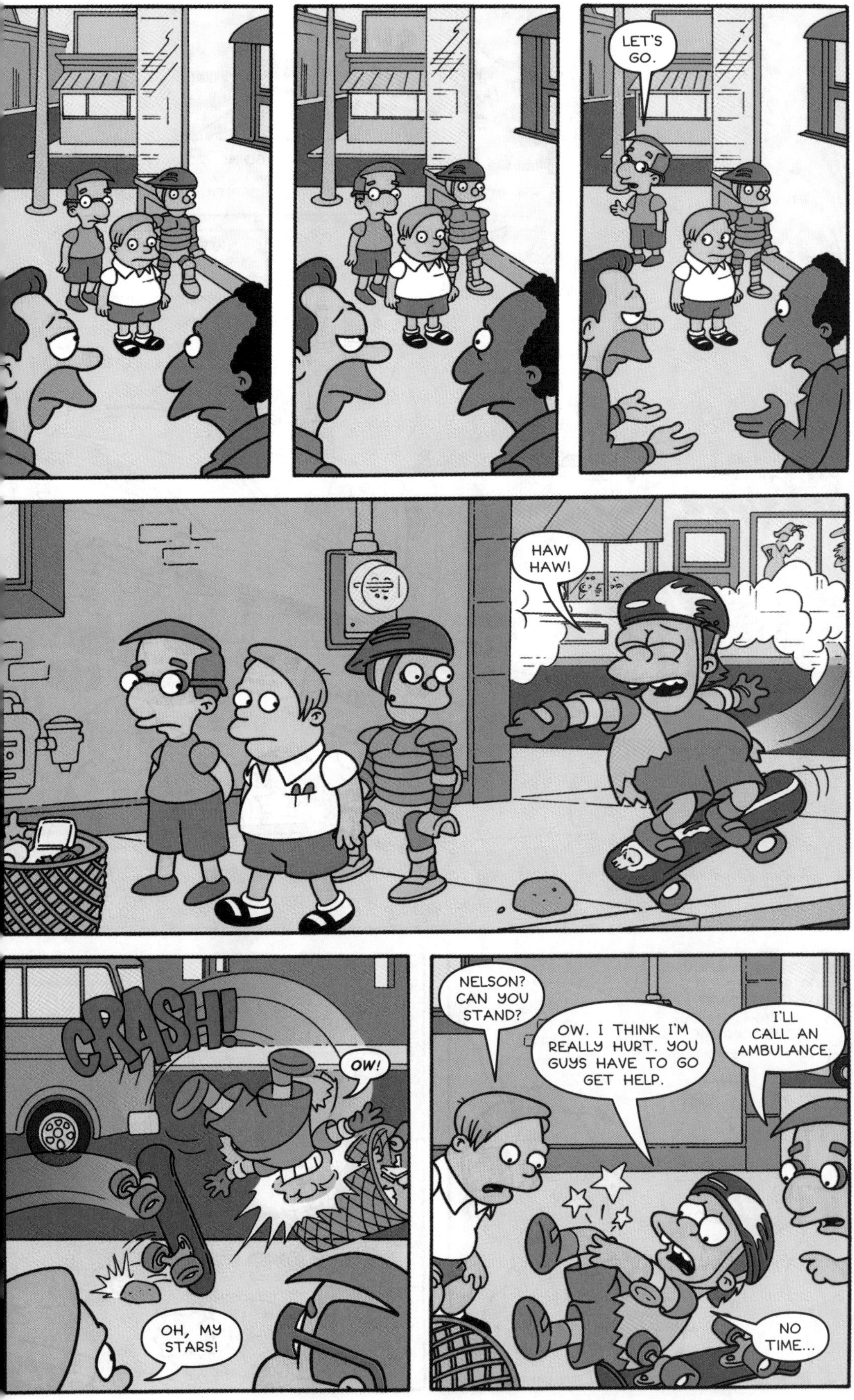
LET'S GO.
HAW HAW!
CRASH!
OW!
OH, MY STARS!
NELSON? CAN YOU STAND?
OW. I THINK I'M REALLY HURT. YOU GUYS HAVE TO GO GET HELP.
I'LL CALL AN AMBULANCE.
NO TIME...

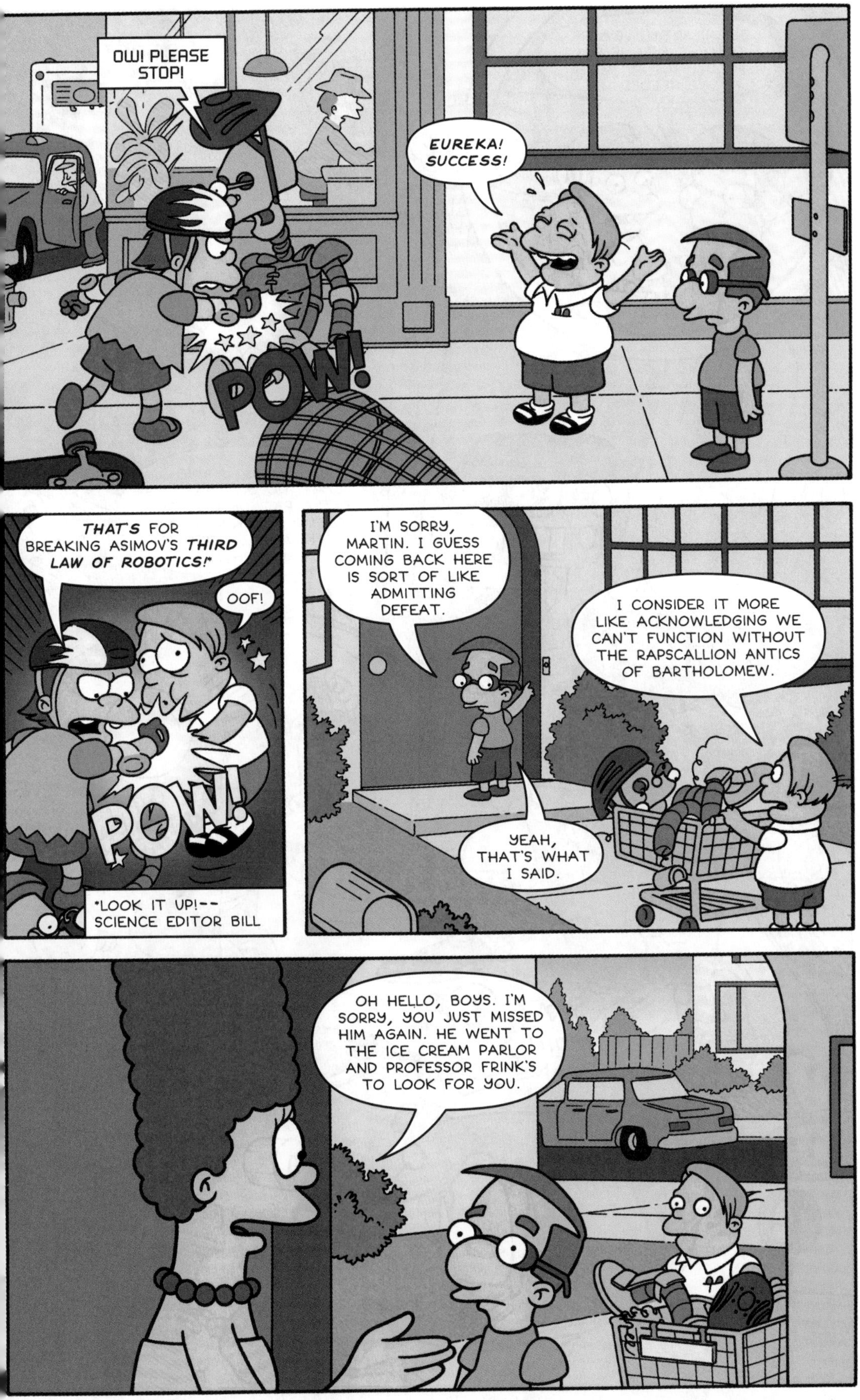

OW! PLEASE STOP!
EUREKA! SUCCESS!
POW!
THAT'S FOR BREAKING ASIMOV'S THIRD LAW OF ROBOTICS!*
OOF!
POW!
*LOOK IT UP!-- SCIENCE EDITOR BILL
I'M SORRY, MARTIN. I GUESS COMING BACK HERE IS SORT OF LIKE ADMITTING DEFEAT.
I CONSIDER IT MORE LIKE ACKNOWLEDGING WE CAN'T FUNCTION WITHOUT THE RAPSCALLION ANTICS OF BARTHOLOMEW.
YEAH, THAT'S WHAT I SAID.
OH HELLO, BOYS. I'M SORRY, YOU JUST MISSED HIM AGAIN. HE WENT TO THE ICE CREAM PARLOR AND PROFESSOR FRINK'S TO LOOK FOR YOU.

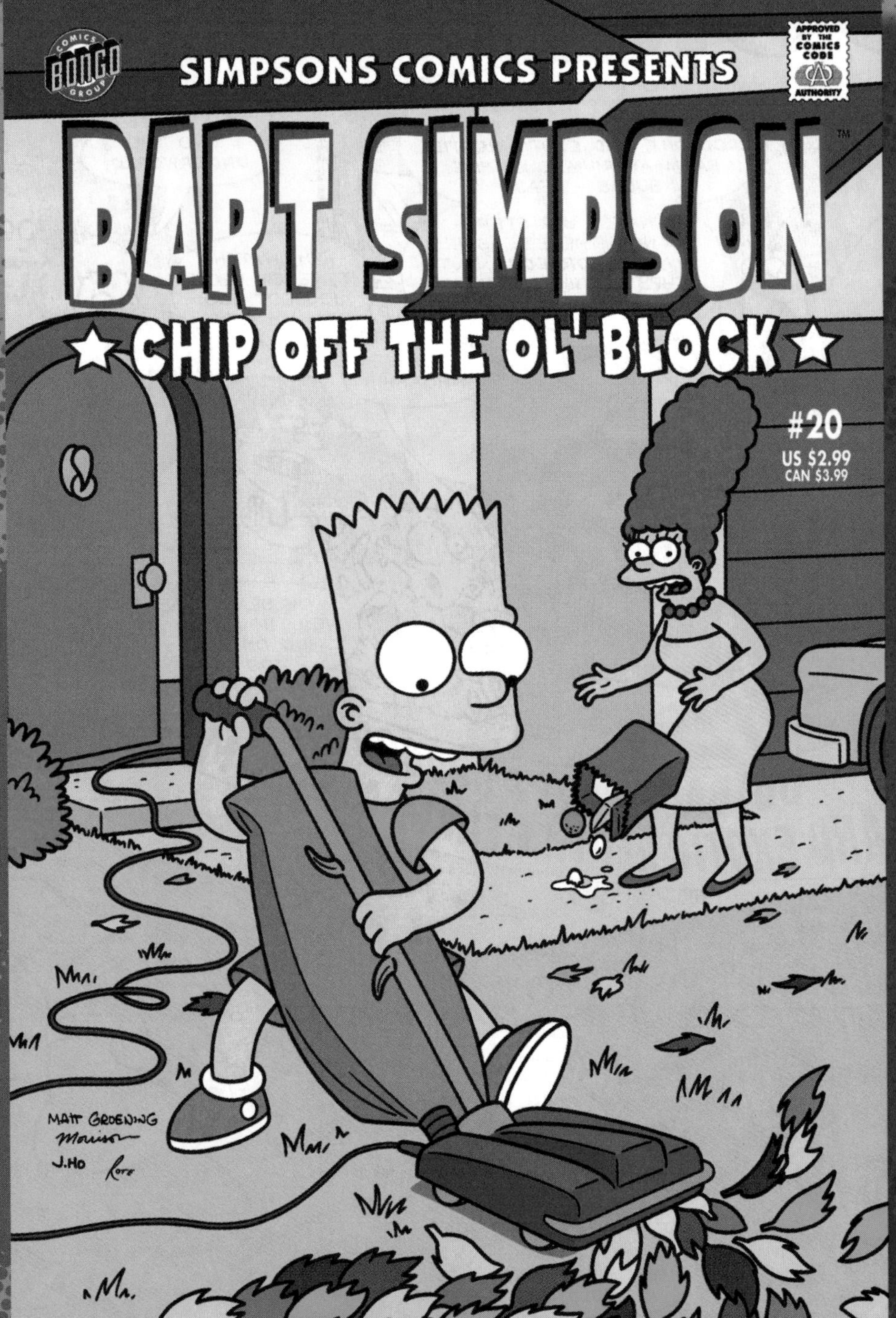

SIMPSONS COMICS PRESENTS
BART SIMPSON
★ CHIP OFF THE OL' BLOCK ★
#20
US $2.99
CAN $3.99
APPROVED BY THE COMICS CODE AUTHORITY
MATT GROENING
J.HO

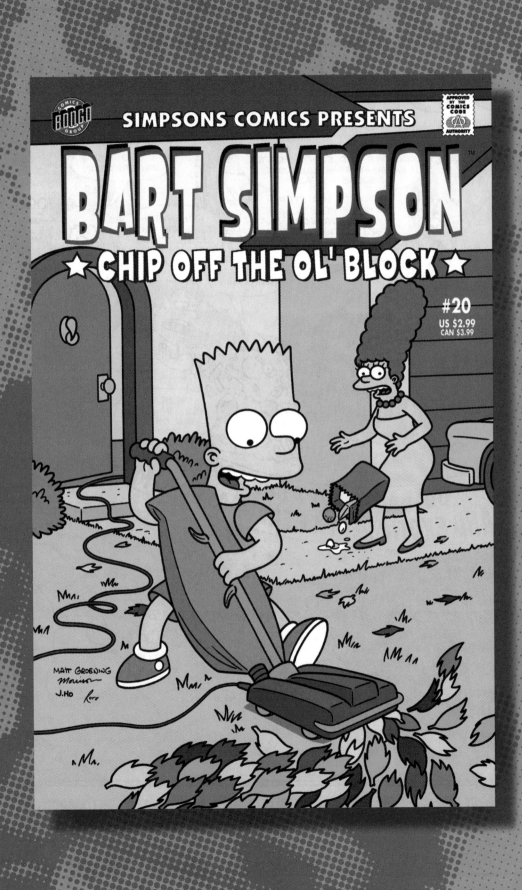

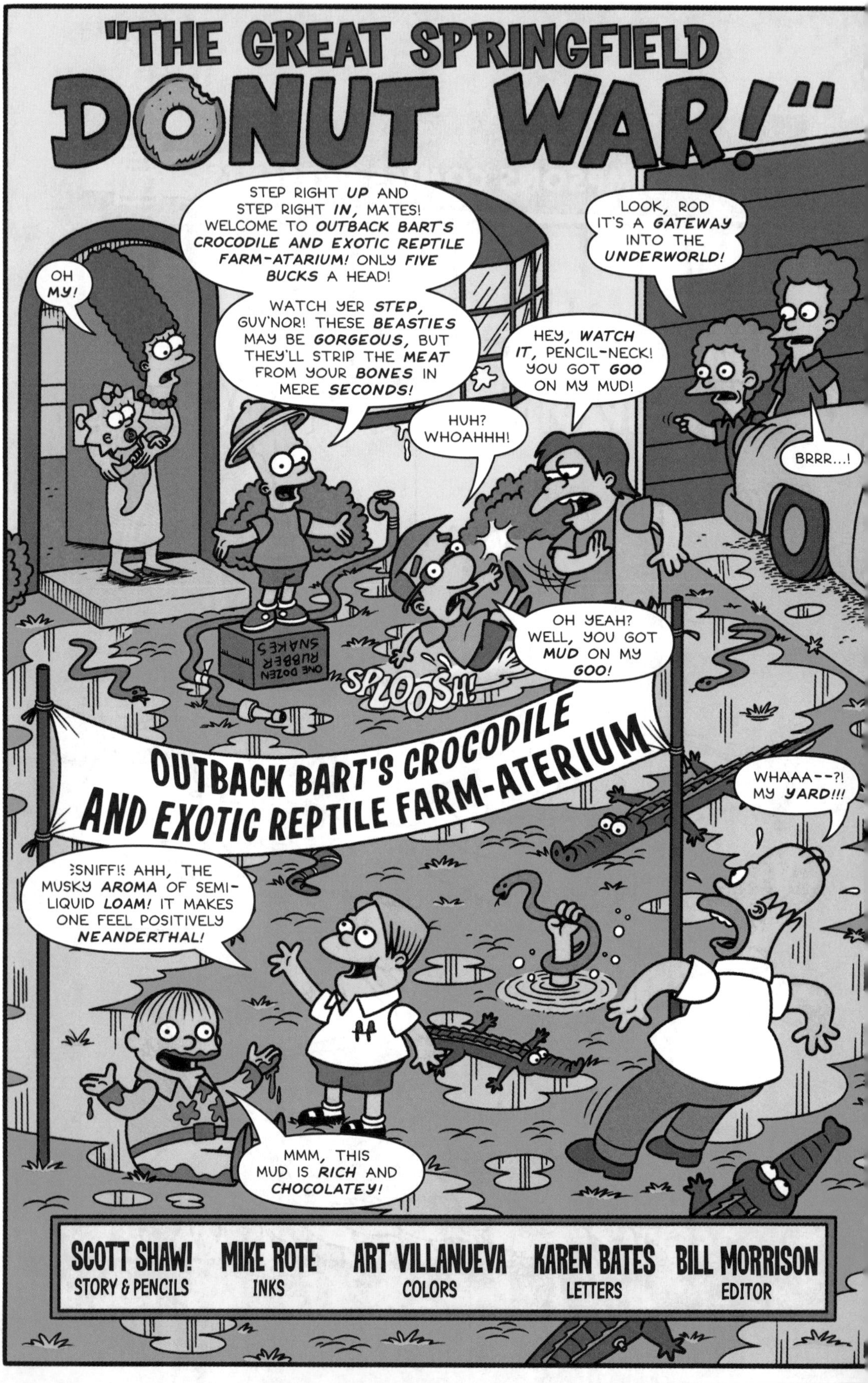
"THE GREAT SPRINGFIELD DONUT WAR!"
OH MY!
STEP RIGHT UP AND STEP RIGHT IN, MATES! WELCOME TO OUTBACK BART'S CROCODILE AND EXOTIC REPTILE FARM-ATARIUM! ONLY FIVE BUCKS A HEAD!
WATCH YER STEP, GUV'NOR! THESE BEASTIES MAY BE GORGEOUS, BUT THEY'LL STRIP THE MEAT FROM YOUR BONES IN MERE SECONDS!
LOOK, ROD IT'S A GATEWAY INTO THE UNDERWORLD!
BRRR...!
HEY, WATCH IT, PENCIL-NECK! YOU GOT GOO ON MY MUD!
HUH? WHOAHHH!
OH YEAH? WELL, YOU GOT MUD ON MY GOO!
ONE DOZEN RUBBER SNAKES
SPLOOSH!
OUTBACK BART'S CROCODILE AND EXOTIC REPTILE FARM-ATERIUM
WHAAA--?! MY YARD!!!
SNIFF! AHH, THE MUSKY AROMA OF SEMI-LIQUID LOAM! IT MAKES ONE FEEL POSITIVELY NEANDERTHAL!
MMM, THIS MUD IS RICH AND CHOCOLATEY!
SCOTT SHAW! STORY & PENCILS
MIKE ROTE INKS
ART VILLANUEVA COLORS
KAREN BATES LETTERS
BILL MORRISON EDITOR

93

94

97

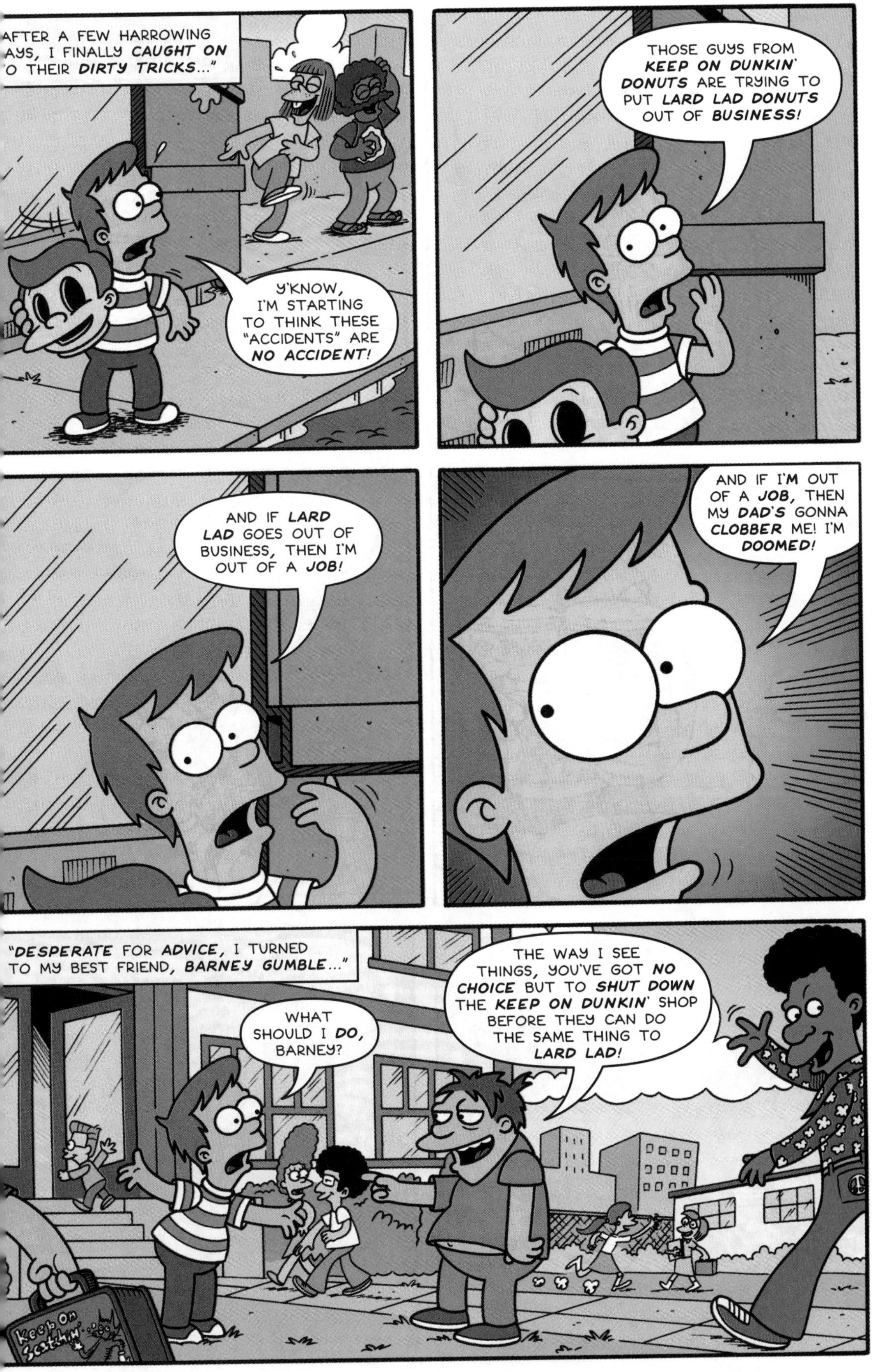
AFTER A FEW HARROWING
AYS, I FINALLY CAUGHT ON
O THEIR DIRTY TRICKS..."
Y'KNOW, I'M STARTING TO THINK THESE "ACCIDENTS" ARE NO ACCIDENT!
THOSE GUYS FROM KEEP ON DUNKIN' DONUTS ARE TRYING TO PUT LARD LAD DONUTS OUT OF BUSINESS!
AND IF LARD LAD GOES OUT OF BUSINESS, THEN I'M OUT OF A JOB!
AND IF I'M OUT OF A JOB, THEN MY DAD'S GONNA CLOBBER ME! I'M DOOMED!
"DESPERATE FOR ADVICE, I TURNED TO MY BEST FRIEND, BARNEY GUMBLE..."
WHAT SHOULD I DO, BARNEY?
THE WAY I SEE THINGS, YOU'VE GOT NO CHOICE BUT TO SHUT DOWN THE KEEP ON DUNKIN' SHOP BEFORE THEY CAN DO THE SAME THING TO LARD LAD!
Keep On Scratchin'

BART'S FUN PAGES PART II

KRUSTY'S COMPUTER-GENERATED CRYPTOGRAM

WHEN YOU'RE AS ILLITERATE AS ME, IT **ALL** LOOKS LIKE THIS.

CRYPTOGRAM INSTRUCTIONS: DECODE THIS TIMELY INSTRUCTION BY CHANGING EACH LETTER TO ITS CORRESPONDING LETTER. THEN DECODE THE AUTHOR'S NAME.

"WVXLWV GSRH GRNVOB RMHGIFXGRLM YI XSZMTRMT VZXS OVGGVI GL RGH XLIIVHKLMWRMT OVGGVI. GSVM WVXLWV GSV ZFGSLIH MZNV."
–XIBKGLTIZN RMHGIFXGRLMH

ANSWER KEY:
A=Z, B=Y, C=X, D=W, E=V, F=U, G=T, H=S, I=R, J=Q, K=P, L=O, M=N

COMIC BOOK GUY'S CATCHPHRASE JUMBLE

I WILL EXPLAIN THIS CHILDISHLY SIMPLE GAME. UNSCRAMBLE THESE WORDS, ONE LETTER TO EACH SQUARE, TO FORM FOUR POPULAR CATCH-PHRASES.

THAT WAS FRUSTRATINGLY DISTASTEFUL.

KOYIN

DYHKEIS

BURACAM

GIMNEBEG

NOW ARRANGE THE CIRCLED LETTERS TO FORM THE ANSWER THAT *I* ALREADY FIGURED OUT WITHOUT THE CLUES ANYWAY BECAUSE PUNS ARE MORE OBVIOUS THAN ANAGRAMS.

WHAT DID HOMER SAY WHEN HE ATE THE UNCOOKED CAKE?

Yoink, Hey kids, Carumba, Embiggen "DOUGH!"

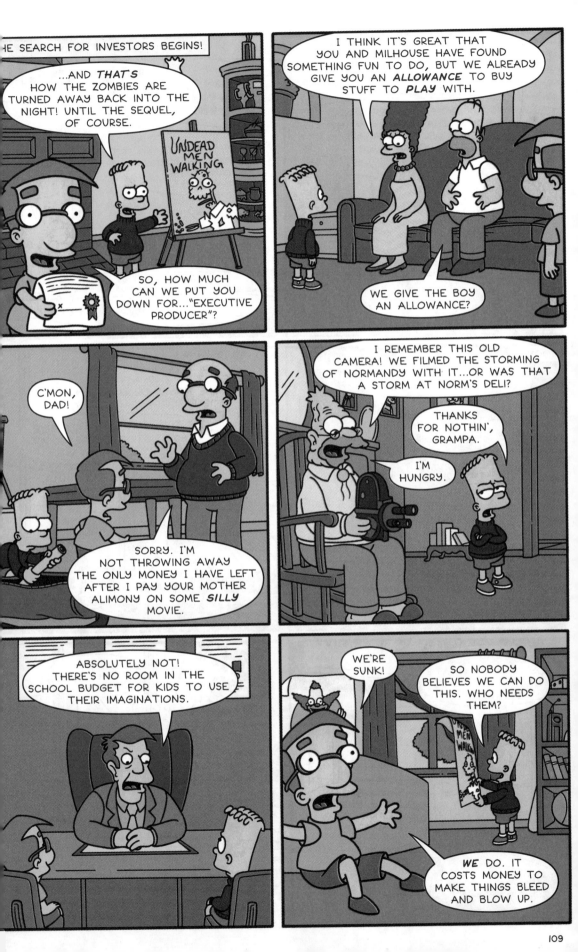

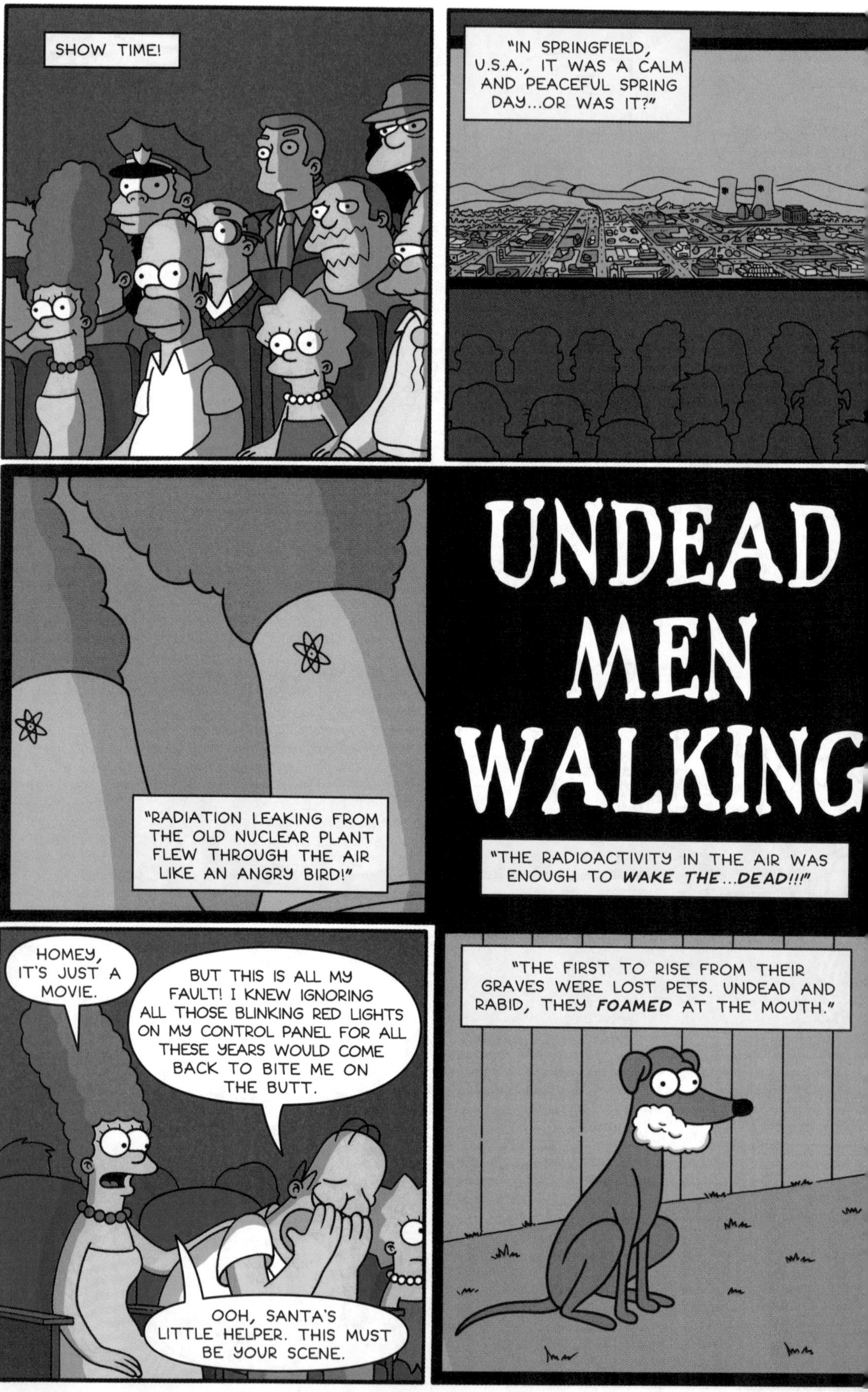
SHOW TIME!
"IN SPRINGFIELD, U.S.A., IT WAS A CALM AND PEACEFUL SPRING DAY...OR WAS IT?"
UNDEAD MEN WALKING
"RADIATION LEAKING FROM THE OLD NUCLEAR PLANT FLEW THROUGH THE AIR LIKE AN ANGRY BIRD!"
"THE RADIOACTIVITY IN THE AIR WAS ENOUGH TO WAKE THE...DEAD!!!"
HOMEY, IT'S JUST A MOVIE.
BUT THIS IS ALL MY FAULT! I KNEW IGNORING ALL THOSE BLINKING RED LIGHTS ON MY CONTROL PANEL FOR ALL THESE YEARS WOULD COME BACK TO BITE ME ON THE BUTT.
OOH, SANTA'S LITTLE HELPER. THIS MUST BE YOUR SCENE.
"THE FIRST TO RISE FROM THEIR GRAVES WERE LOST PETS. UNDEAD AND RABID, THEY FOAMED AT THE MOUTH."

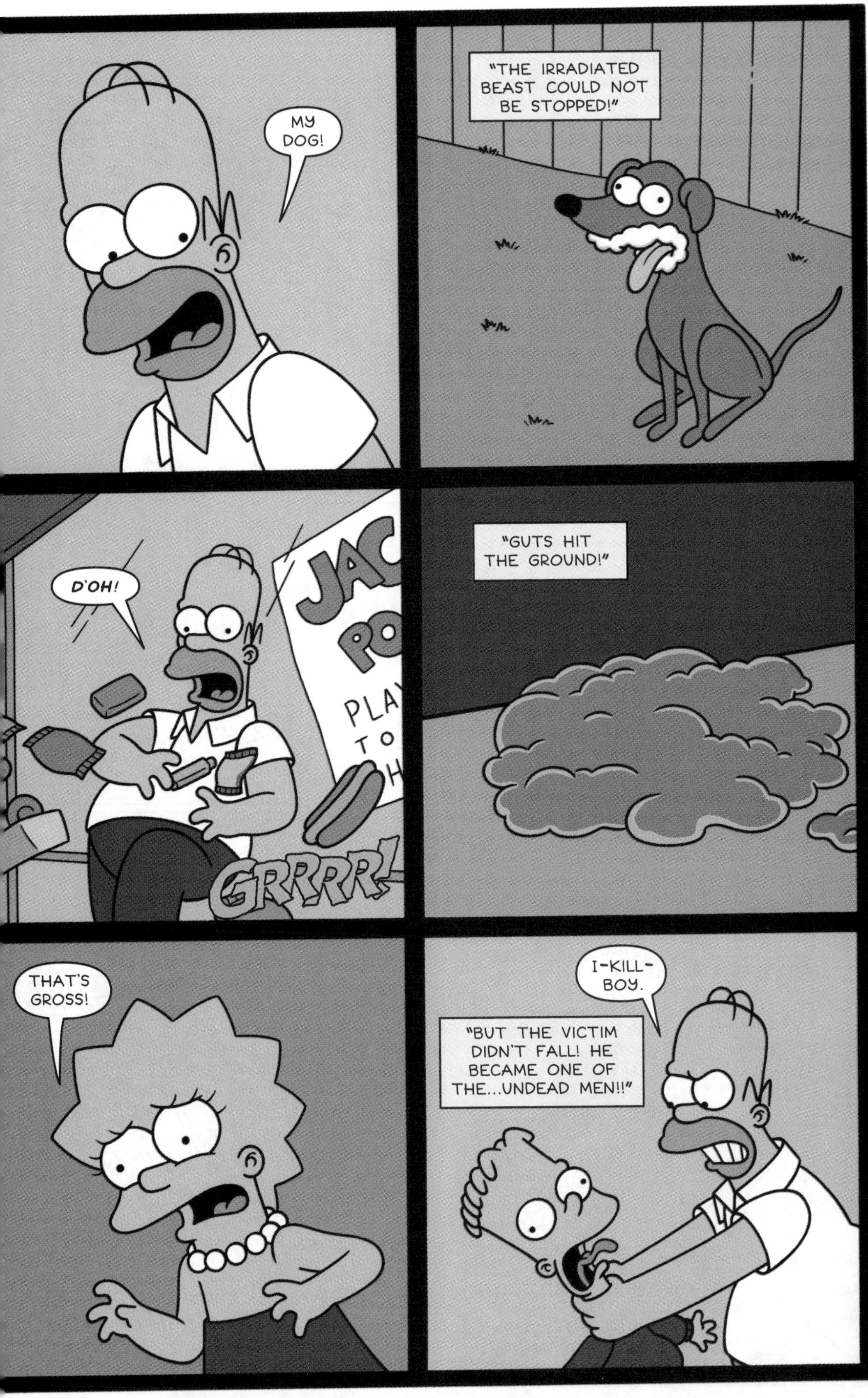
MY DOG!
"THE IRRADIATED BEAST COULD NOT BE STOPPED!"
D'OH!
GRRRR!
"GUTS HIT THE GROUND!"
THAT'S GROSS!
"BUT THE VICTIM DIDN'T FALL! HE BECAME ONE OF THE...UNDEAD MEN!!"
I-KILL-BOY.